THE HOUSE DIVIDED

THE STORY OF THE FIRST CONGRESSIONAL BASEBALL GAME

J.B. MANHEIM

SUNBURY
PRESS

Mechanicsburg, PA USA

Published by Sunbury Press, Inc.
Mechanicsburg, Pennsylvania

SUNBURY
P R E S S
www.sunburypress.com

For information about special discounts for bulk purchases, please contact Sunbury Press Orders Dept. at (855) 338-8359 or orders@sunburypress.com.

To request one of our authors for speaking engagements or book signings, please contact Sunbury Press Publicity Dept. at publicity@sunburypress.com.

FIRST SUNBURY PRESS EDITION: April 2025

Set in Adobe Garamond | Interior design by Crystal Devine | Cover by Lawrence Knorr | Edited by Lawrence Knorr.

Publisher's Cataloging-in-Publication Data
Names: Manheim, J.B., author.
Title: The house divided : the story of the first congressional baseball game / J.B. Manheim.
Description: First trade paperback edition. | Mechanicsburg, PA : Sunbury Press, 2025.
Summary: 1909. Congress is immersed in a classic struggle involving special interests, ideology, personal animosity, partisanship, and a great deal of money, all presided over by a tyrannical leader with an agenda. As pressure on the Hill builds in the summer heat a safety valve is needed: a baseball game. Baseball as recreational sport. Politics as blood sport. That's our tale. And by the end literally everything has changed.
Identifiers: ISBN 979-8-88819-285-6 (softcover).
Subjects: HISTORY / United States / 20th Century | SPORTS & RECREATION / Baseball / History | POLITICAL SCIENCE / American Government / Legislative Branch.

Designed in the USA
0 1 1 2 3 5 8 13 21 34 55

For the Love of Books!

Here's One More for Amy.
After All These Years
She Still Bats 1.000.

ALSO BY J.B. MANHEIM

FICTION
The Deadball Files

Book 1
This Never Happened:
The Mystery Behind the Death of Christy Mathewson

Book 2
The Gamekeepers:
Whitewash, Blackmail, and Baseball's Darkest Secrets

Book 3
Doubleday Doubletake:
One Ball, Three Strikes, One Man Out

Book 4
The Federal Case

Book 5
The Keystone Corner:
Thomas Edison Turns Two

Book 6
Field of Schemes

SELECTED NONFICTION

Strategy in Information and Influence Campaigns:
How Policy Advocates, Social Movements, Insurgent Groups,
Corporations, Governments and Others Get What They Want

WITH LAWRENCE KNORR

What's in Ted's Wallet?
The Newly Revealed T206 Baseball Card Collection
of Thomas Edison's Youngest Son

TABLE OF CONTENTS

In most years since 1909, Democrats and Republicans on Capitol Hill have squared off in a good-natured contest—the Congressional Baseball Game. Once a modest affair, the event now draws close to thirty thousand fans and raises more than a million dollars annually for local charities. This is the story of the very first Congressional Baseball Game.

"Politics are almost as exciting as war, and quite as dangerous. In war you can only be killed once, but in politics many times."

— ATTRIBUTED TO WINSTON CHURCHILL[1]

*

"The secret to managing is to keep the guys who hate you away from the guys who are undecided."

— CASEY STENGEL[2]

*

"Baseball is the nation's safety valve."

— ALLEN SANGREE[3]

THIS FIELD, THIS GAME

EVERY BASEBALL SEASON brings its share of generally inconsequential, colorful, and quirky events that tickle the fancy of fans of the game when they occur but are then lost to the collective memory.[1] Nineteen-nine was no exception. Three particular examples come to mind.

The first of these we might call the balloon fly. Normally, the term "balloon fly" refers to an unusually high fly ball, but perhaps not always. On June 5, 1909, the first annual National Balloon Race was launched from the Indianapolis Motor Speedway, the first event ever at the speedway, which drew some forty thousand fans more than two months before the track itself was completed. The "race" was actually a test of performance, endurance, control, direction, and distance for hot air balloons that was serving, among other things, as a test of their military applications (paralleling those of the Wright brothers and Glen Curtiss for powered flight that we will encounter later in our tale). After release, the balloons traveled helter-skelter across several states at the mercy of the winds. Days later, while heading home to St. Louis, one of the balloons, named *Melba*, piloted by John Berry and M.A. Helmann, was blown off its planned course by a thunderstorm. In the last inning of a baseball game in Wrights, Illinois, north of St. Louis, with the home team up by one and visiting Kankakee at bat, the star batter for the visitors came to the plate with two on and two outs. He hit a lazy fly ball that was within easy reach of the left fielder. Unfortunately, *Melba* passed directly over the ballpark at that very moment with its anchor rope dragging along the ground. The rope struck the left fielder and knocked him down just as he reached for the ball. The fielder and the ball hit the turf, and the batter raced around the bases for a three-run home run. Reportedly, the local fans swarmed out of the bleachers in a fury, intending to capture the drag line and pull the balloon to the ground, where they might wreak vengeance on the offending aeronauts. It was only in the nick of time that the racers managed to release their remaining ballast and shoot upward and out of harm's way.[2] The one thing we can say with assurance about the batter himself is that his name was not Casey Stengel. It was not until the following year, 1910, that first-year outfielder Stengel, age nineteen, played for the Kankakee Kanks in the Class D Northern Association.

The second only-in-baseball event happened about a month later in a New York State League contest between the Albany Senators and the Syracuse Stars. The Stars had runners on first and third with one out when they attempted a double steal, a classic move designed to draw a throw to second that would allow the runner at third to score. Anticipating the play, the Albany pitcher threw the ball instead to third base, which caused the runner there to dive back to the bag but also prompted the runner at first, already primed to be running, to head for second. The third baseman threw to second, forcing the first-base runner to retreat. When the second baseman threw to first, hoping to catch the retreating runner, the runner at third set off for home. He was turned back by the first baseman's throw to the catcher and caught in a rundown, while the runner from first took second and kept going. This went on for no fewer than eighteen throws involving eight of the nine Albany fielders, and in the end, *both* runners were tagged out, one by the left fielder and one by the center fielder, which is to say, it resulted in what was then and may still be today the most complicated double play in baseball history.[3] The *Washington Post* captured the play in the graphic in Figure 1.

But it is the third of these 1909 sporting odds and ends that will be our focus here. For sandwiched neatly between the balloon fly and that dilly of a pickle, and in its own way of a piece with both, was the very first congressional baseball game. As a shorthand, let's call that the CBG, and more particularly CBG1.

CBG1 had two of the earmarks of a classic only-in-baseball moment. It was colorful and it was most assuredly quirky. Picture a dozen and a half forty-year-old (plus or minus) men, out of shape and, in many

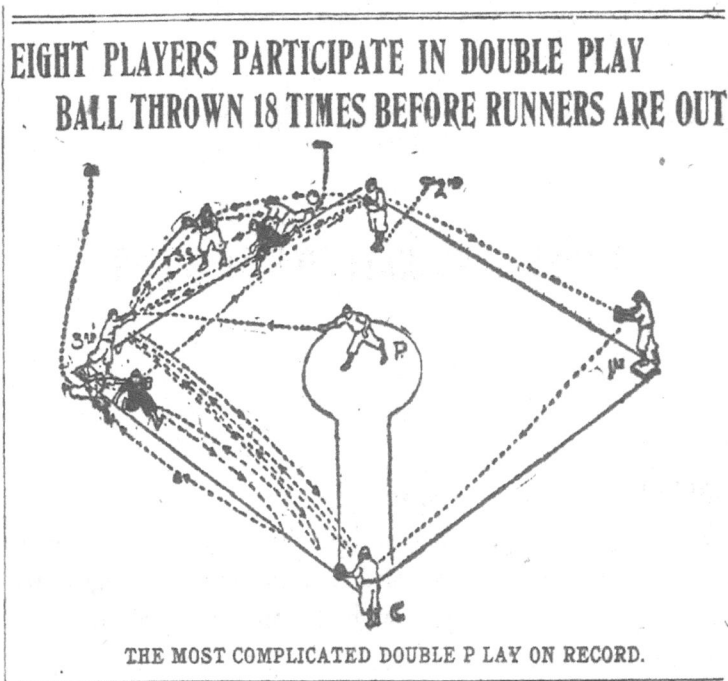

EIGHT PLAYERS PARTICIPATE IN DOUBLE PLAY
BALL THROWN 18 TIMES BEFORE RUNNERS ARE OUT

THE MOST COMPLICATED DOUBLE P LAY ON RECORD.

Figure 1. Charting the biggest pickle in baseball history (1909).

instances, well beyond their playing weight, dressed in all manner of sporting attire and cavorting around a major league ballpark as if they knew what they were doing. That was CBG1.

But the game lacked that one additional characteristic of the type, for it was not by any means inconsequential—at least not in its intent. CBG1 was part of a deadly serious political struggle over what until recently we would have come to regard as an obscure issue, the tariffs set by the United States on international trade, that in the end had impacts on the way that Congress does its business and on the citizens that business is presumed to serve, both of which redound to this very day.

Baseball as a recreational sport. Politics as a blood sport. These are the elements of our tale. Without further ado, let us begin.

THREE GUYS WALKED INTO A BAR

WELL, NOT EXACTLY. So, let's try again.

Eight guys—six congressmen and two lobbyists, to be precise—piled into a pair of 1909 touring cars and set out from Washington to Baltimore to attend a minor league baseball game. They could have stayed in town and done the same thing—and watched a major league game instead if one could truly classify the Washington Nationals of 1909 as a major league team—without the hassles of intercity travel. But that would not have suited their purposes.

On June 22, John Tener, a first-term Republican from Pennsylvania, called his old friend Ned Hanlon, president of the Baltimore Orioles of the Eastern League, to arrange a visit. Tener was a former major league pitcher and teammate of Hanlon's during the latter's playing days. He told Hanlon that he planned to come to the next day's game in Baltimore against the Montreal Royals accompanied by a three-car delegation of congressmen and other dignitaries who wanted a weekend escape from the debate over tariffs. Hanlon, in turn, made the planned visit public in the expectation that it would generate local excitement in Baltimore. It did accomplish that, and the local media even described the visiting delegation as "statesmen," a sobriquet that today we would scarcely expect to see applied to a cohort of visiting congressmen.

Hanlon may have planted the idea for this sojourn earlier in June when he was in the capital for a matchup between the Senators and the Detroit Tigers, though if so, it is not clear with whom he may have been speaking. Tener said he expected to bring eleven companions including

Congressmen Edward Vreeland, Sereno Payne, and John J. Fitzgerald, all of New York, as well as five other members of the House—Ralph Cole of Ohio, Charles Townsend of Michigan, Thomas Butler of Pennsylvania, Joseph Gaines of West Virginia, and J. W. Byrns of Tennessee (together with Fitzgerald the only Democrats in the group)—retired Congressman James Watson, former Senator James Hemenway of Indiana, and Judge J.B. Fisher of Jamestown, New York.[1]

It is a revealing list. Payne was both Majority Leader and Chairman of the Ways and Means Committee, an extraordinary combination of power centers that one never sees these days, and he was the primary sponsor of the version of tariff reform then pending before the House of Representatives. Gaines was also a member of Ways and Means, while Fitzgerald was cast in the role of a rebellious Democrat, having sided with the Speaker of the House, Joe Cannon, and against his own party in a battle earlier in the session over the rules for conducting House business. He had been rewarded with an appointment to the powerful Rules Committee over the objections of the Democratic leadership. Watson, formerly the Republican whip, the party leader responsible for wrangling votes and maintaining discipline, was an advocate on tariff matters with ties to the National Association of Manufacturers, a strongly protectionist business group. In January 1909, Payne had turned to him for assistance in reining in a fellow Hoosier, Congressman Edgar Crumpacker, the one Republican on the Ways and Means Committee who seemed to favor free trade over protectionist tariffs.[2] Hemenway was a strong protectionist who had just lost his seat in the Senate to a reform advocate, a decision made by the Indiana state legislature at the urging of the governor after a protracted consideration of the tariff issue.[3] Fisher, though he retained the title, was no longer a member of the judiciary but was, instead, a lobbyist for the oil and gas industry and yet another strong advocate of protectionist tariffs.[4] But for Mr. Byrns, the other members of Congress on the list were Republican allies of Mr. Payne and reliable votes on the tariff. Byrns was a tariff reformer all the way, but it may have been his friendship and alliance with Congressman Gaines that led to his inclusion in the group. Byrns and Gaines were among a coalition in the House that had pressed for repeal of a tax on raw leaf tobacco, a provision that was included in the bill that would eventually emerge from Ways and

Means and survive in the Senate.[5] Or perhaps Byrns was being used as a bridge to the Democratic leadership. We cannot know.

One mystery ought to be noted in this list. Mr. Fitzgerald, the rebel Democrat, is described in the *Baltimore Sun* article announcing the expected visit as follows: "Mr. Fitzgerald is one of the best friends Mr. Hanlon has. He was a catcher on the Brooklyn National League team, and even after he was coaxed out of the game and into politics and finally into Congress. . . . [his] name is familiar to nearly all followers of the game."[6] The mystery arises because, though he did play the game in college, as we will see, neither the Baseball Reference database nor any press account that I was able to locate refers to a player matching that name and description ever having played in professional baseball in either the major or the minor leagues.

In the event, however, Fitzgerald did not make the trip. Neither did Vreeland, who was scheduled to address the Maryland State Bankers' Association at the Blue Mountain House resort in Western Maryland the following evening and may already have departed for distant Hagerstown,[7] or Hemenway. The plan was for the remaining dignitaries to depart from the Willard Hotel in Washington at one o'clock in the afternoon and make the drive to Baltimore, arriving at the Belvedere Hotel, from whence Mr. Hanlon would escort the group to the ballpark. Alas, things did not work out that way.

The drive was expected to last two hours, which would place the visitors at the rendezvous point around three in the afternoon. Game time was at four. In the words of the *National Tribune*,

> Last Wednesday, one of the most blisteringist [*sic*] hot days of the Summer, a big automobile skinned away into the country for a run to Baltimore. The "joy riders" were going over to see a baseball game between the Orioles and Montreal. The people in the automobile will none of them see 50 again, and most of them would be glad to say they hoped to welcome 60, while two at least were on the shadow side of that "tie."[8]

In reality, two automobiles headed north that afternoon. They did not have an easy time of it. Today, there are three principal direct routes from Washington to Baltimore, including Interstate 95 and the Balti-more-Washington Parkway, both of them limited access roadways, and US Highway 1, as well as any number of less direct connections. But in 1909, travel between the neighboring cities required navigating a network of county roads that were generally neither well-marked nor well-maintained. Though the Maryland General Assembly had begun to appropriate funds for State Road 1, a boulevard linking the two, in 1909, the traveler still encountered unpaved sections and bone-rattling grade crossings.[9] Such roads provided a stern test of any automobile intended to cover forty miles, let alone a pair of big touring cars moving in tan-dem. But that was the challenge the traveling party took on.

One auto carried Payne, Butler, Gaines, and Fisher, while the other held Tener, Townsend, Byrns, and Cole. (Watson is reported to have attended the game as well, but how he got there is not clear.) There is no record as to who was driving. The trip went as planned until the caravan reached Laurel, Maryland, roughly the halfway point, where the bearings of the vehicle carrying the Tener group overheated. Members of the party were forced to sun themselves while they waited for the bearings to cool. Once they were again on their way, they hit a stretch of bad road and were forced to slow down considerably. Then, about a mile from the Baltimore city line, the same troublesome auto broke down completely, stranding the occupants. Payne and his group continued to the Belvedere, arriving around 4:15, a mere hour and a quarter behind schedule. Their would-be host, Ned Hanlon, handed the group over to his son, who saw them to the directors' boxes at Oriole Park. In the meantime, Hanlon himself drove out to rescue the second group, which he then stewarded to the ballpark in time for the start of the fifth inning.

Once at the game, Butler, Cole, and Tener were reported to be the most enthusiastic rooters, yelling, groaning, and even shouting at the umpires. For his part, Payne was credited with displaying a deep knowledge of the game, and especially of the pitching, fielding, and strategic deficiencies of the Washington Nationals team, which were manifold. Following the game, the visitors were treated to a celebratory dinner back on the roof garden of the Belvedere Hotel, the city's newest and finest. Then, around nine in the evening, it was back to Washington, with Hanlon again pro-viding transportation for the group whose auto had broken down.[10]

Figure 2. Oriole Park IV (1909).

Apparently, and given the company, not surprisingly, not all of the conversation at the ballpark centered on the game at hand. No. The topic of the day was the tariff. Indeed, the group was described by the local press as a cluster of "tariff experts." True to form, all of the Republicans except Payne, who refused to discuss the subject publicly, made a point of claiming that the new tariff bill would result in significant downward revisions in the rates. As we will see, this messaging was part of a cynical strategy that was playing out both in public and on Capitol Hill—talk the reform talk, walk the protectionist walk. Do the former in public, do the latter behind tightly closed doors. Messrs. Cole and Butler went further, suggesting that a corporation or inheritance tax, both favored by reform-minded progressives and Democrats, might be passed to offset the loss of government income that would accompany lower duties, but neither made reference to another proposed tax measure favored by the reformers, a constitutional amendment to allow the government to claim a share of the income of individual citizens, that had been proposed by President Taft the previous week and would be introduced in the House and the Senate just a few days later. Only the lone Democrat, Mr. Byrns, not privy to the strategy and certainly not friendly to its objective, claimed the revision of tariffs would be upward, that is, even more skewed toward protectionism. Byrns simply asserted, "I feel confident that the people will be disappointed" with the new tariff schedules.[11]

It is almost a certainty that this visit to Oriole Park in late June was connected in some way with the idea of pitting congressional Democrats and Republicans against one another on a baseball diamond in

Washington barely three weeks later, something that, notwithstanding the long histories of both the Congress and baseball in the nation's capital, had never been done before. The timing of such a consideration was certainly propitious. At the very end of 1907—December 30, to be precise—Abraham Mills, chairman of the eponymous Mills Commission that had been appointed by the prominent baseball personality and sporting goods mogul Albert Spalding to identify the originator of America's game, had written to James Edward Sullivan, president of the Amateur Athletic Union and secretary of the commission, advising of his conclusion that one Abner Doubleday had invented the game in Cooperstown, New York, in 1839.[12] Both men were Spalding "insiders," and Spalding himself had reached this "conclusion"—eventually, of course, judged false—months earlier, in September of that year, referencing Doubleday as the inventor at a gathering in Cleveland on the twenty-first[13] before reporting in New York five days later that

> The first authentic record I have been able to secure dates the commencement of baseball in America to 1839, when a youth of Cooperstown, N.Y., Abner Doubleday by name, outlined the diamond field in the dirt with a stick and explained the game to his boy playmates, and afterward drew up a set of playing rules for this new game, which he called baseball.[14]

As we saw above, Allen Sangree was already waxing philosophical in the nation's magazines about the benefit of baseball as a means of relieving the tensions in American society, also in 1907.[15] Coincidentally, in May of the following year, articles by both Spalding and Sangree appeared in the second-ever issue of *Baseball Magazine*.[16]

In this light, it is possible, even perhaps natural, that one purpose of the Baltimore trip was to make plans for such a game. A more compelling argument may be that the visit to Baltimore simply planted the idea for the game. Whichever was the case, the timing was too close to have been merely coincidental, and it is noteworthy that three of the travelers—Messrs. Cole, Gaines, and Tener—played in that game, while one of the no-shows, Mr. Vreeland, was set to do the same but for a last-minute injury.

Most contemporary observers have concluded that both ventures—the Baltimore trip and the first CBG—were personally conceived by Tener simply as baseball-related diversions. As a former major league pitcher newly arrived in the House John Tener seems a natural protagonist to whom to attribute the origins of the congressional contest. However, this assumption may be too easily reached and may ignore significant elements of the context in which both events occurred. As with many events when viewed only through the backward-looking lens of history, it may be too simple an explanation.

There is at least a very strong circumstantial case to be made suggesting that, while Tener played an important role in this enterprise, it was a more limited one, not as the father of CBG1 but as a convenient *proximate agent* of the congressional leadership who sought to organize both activities for their own purposes. In this view, John Tener was not necessarily the driving force behind either activity for the simple reason that mere diversion was not their goal. There was too much at stake.

ENTER TENER

IN 1888, JOHN TENER, a journeyman pitcher for the Chicago White Stockings of the National League, was selected by Albert Spalding, owner of the club, to be one of two pitchers who would accompany the team on a post-season world exhibition tour that visited twenty-three countries, including destinations as diverse as Australia, Ceylon, the Pacific Islands, and the major capitals of Europe. During the stop in England, Spalding also selected Tener to explain the nuances of baseball to the Prince of Wales, the future King Edward VII, who attended a "match" at the Kennington Oval cricket ground on March 12.[1] The *Manchester Guardian* newspaper provided this description of our national pastime.

> The American base-ball teams who have just arrived in this country begin their short tour with a match in London on Tuesday . . . [T]he game will be played at its highest perfection by the gentlemen who constitute the teams, and we shall be able to say whether or not a formidable rival to cricket has appeared among us . . . The physique of these athletes is worthy of notice, the majority of them standing close upon six feet in height . . . The ground on which the game of base-ball is played is marked out in the shape of a diamond, the sides being 90 feet in length. A canvas bag filled with horsehair is placed at each corner, and these are distinguished by the terms 1st, 2nd, and 3rd base and home plate. The bowler, or, as he is called in this game, the pitcher, stands in a space 4 feet wide by 5 feet 4 inches long, situated in

the centre of the diamond. This place is known as the pitcher's box, and is 50 feet distant from the home plate, where the batsman stands . . . The theory of the game is that two contesting teams must endeavour to send the greater number of men round the circuit of the bases under the rules prescribed within a limited number of innings . . . The batsman endeavours to hit the ball so that it will pass the intercepting fielders and go to such distance as will enable him to reach the first base before the ball can be returned to the fielder stationed there . . . The Americans claim for their national game that there is more dash, more enterprise, more "git up and git" to it in a minute than anything else of the kind in the world . . .[2]

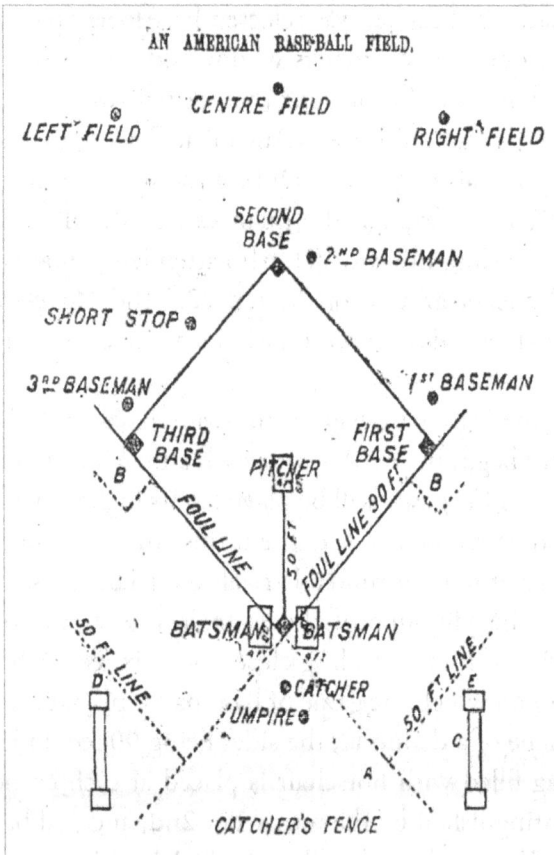

Figure 3. The English view of baseball.

The same article went on to note the following.

> Mr. John K. Tener is the Chicago pitcher (or bowler), and his delivery of the ball once seen is not likely to be soon forgotten. Indeed, it seems to exercise a kind of fascination upon the spectator.[3]

The delivery to which the newspaper referred was Tener's curveball. In a fit of the overstatement to which American newspapers of the day were prone, the *Lancaster Inquirer* later described Tener's effectiveness during the tour thus:

> Tener was one of the first great American pitchers, and he showed the royalty and nobility of Europe what a strong man can do with a little horsehide sphere. To them it was like the legerdemain of the conjurers of India. They saw him twirl his long arms above his head, writhe his long body into position and force the little sphere to describe arcs in the air in apparent defiance of the laws of gravity. It was their introduction to the curved ball . . .[4]

Given that his record in a mere two seasons with the White Stockings was 22 wins and 20 losses, followed by a single year in the breakaway Players League in which he won 3 games while losing 11 and pitched to an ERA of 7.21, it is a reach to characterize John Tener as "one of the first great American pitchers." Nevertheless, when he arrived on Capitol Hill twenty years later, his status as a former major league pitcher and his glossily remembered fame from the Spalding World Tour, which had garnered a great deal of publicity across the country, helped to mark him as a standout of sorts when he came on the Washington scene among a class of new freshman members of the Sixty-First Congress in 1909.

John Kinley Tener had a difficult childhood, but one that was perhaps not atypical for his times. The seventh of ten children, Tener was born in County Tyrone, Ireland, in 1863. His parents, George and Susan, were prosperous farmers. When his father died of pneumonia in 1873, his mother moved the family to Pittsburgh to join her oldest daughter, but she passed away that same year. That left young John an orphan to be raised by his older siblings, principally his brother George, Jr. He attended the local public schools, then completed one business college course, whereupon he was hired by an iron and steel manufacturing firm, Lewis, Oliver & Phillips, as a clerk. He stayed with the firm for about five years, during which time he also developed his talent at baseball, an interest he had first discovered at age nine.[5]

In 1885, at age twenty-one, Tener left home to pursue a career in the game, signing on as a coach, pitcher, and outfielder with a professional team representing Haverhill, Massachusetts, in the independent New England League. While there, he met his future first wife, Harriett Day, whom he married in 1889. Among Tener's teammates in Haverhill were future Hall of Famers Wilbert Robertson and Tommy McCarthy, as well as future Supreme Court Justice William H. Moody, who also owned a share of the team. The team was successful on the field but less so at the box office, and midway through the season the directors saw the need to reduce expenses by firing the two highest-paid players, Tener, who earned $125 per month, and future Cincinnati scout Tom McCarthy, who earned $100. The decisive meeting concluded at eleven at night, and the pair were let go before midnight—apparently to save a day's pay. In effect, then, Moody, who concurred in the decision, helped to fire Tener from his first job in baseball. Still, the two remained on friendly terms. Tener then caught on with another New England League team from Lawrence, Massachusetts, to finish out the minor league season, and even played in one game for the Baltimore Orioles of the American Association, considered in 1885 to be a major league, going hitless in four plate appearances.[6]

At that point, Tener returned to the Pittsburgh area, taking a position as secretary of the Charleroi Valley Gas Company. But he retained his love of baseball and played the sandlot game with the Pittsburgh Athletic amateur team. Uncommonly tall at six-feet-four and a compact one hundred eighty pounds, in 1888, he caught the eye of Cap Anson of the Chicago White Stockings of the National League, who signed him to a contract as a pitcher, outfielder, and occasional first baseman. In two years with the team, Tener proved to be a mediocre pitcher, his 22-20 record accompanied by a respectable earned run average of 3.40. In fifty-four games with the White Stockings, he batted .255.

The highlight of those years was undoubtedly the aforementioned world tour. Early on in the adventure, Spalding discovered Tener's business acumen and appointed him as treasurer and personal secretary of the enterprise. And at the conclusion of the journey, Spalding even offered him a position with his company in New York, no doubt impressed by the fact that Tener's accounting over many weeks, across many countries, and through the associated series of complex currency exchanges, when audited at the conclusion of the venture was accurate within seven cents (a surplus).[7]

Incidentally, it was around the conclusion of this tour that Spalding and English-born sportswriter Henry Chadwick began their initially good-natured debate over the origins of baseball, with Spalding proclaiming the game as inherently American and Chadwick claiming its origin in the English game of rounders. Some fifteen years later, this increasingly acrimonious debate would lead to Spalding's campaign to attribute the invention of baseball to American hero Abner Doubleday. Consider, then, the following excerpt from a description in the English press of the Kennington Oval contest:

> Here at least was a good deal more elaborate preparation than was ever to be seen in the old game of rounders, to which baseball has often been compared in England. The result showed that beyond hitting the ball and running the bases the American game has little resemblance to that old-fashioned pastime, or at any rate that it has, with Transatlantic freedom, quite outgrown its prototype.[8]

Throughout his life, the outgoing and gregarious Tener collected friends like some people collect baseball cards. One of those was John Montgomery Ward, who captained the All-Americans, the team opposing the White Stockings on the tour, and who was also the driving force behind the Baseball Brotherhood, a sort of players union. Tener became secretary of the Brotherhood and, as noted, following his second season with Chicago, joined members of the group in forming the Players League, an ill-starred rebellion against the dominant powers in baseball, in 1890. He was recruited away from Chicago by another friend he had made on the tour, Ned Hanlon. The pair played for the Pittsburgh entry in the league, with Tener pitching and Hanlon serving as player-manager. True to form, Tener took on the additional role of financial secretary and treasurer for the club, but his on-field performance left much to be desired.[9]

Much of the business of the Players League, particularly as it related to allocating among the teams those players they might encourage to jump over from the National League, was conducted by telegram using a secret cipher in which National League players were assigned the names of animals, and those available to be signed by the Players League clubs the names of objects. Team managers and the league secretary, Frank Brunell, were thus able to conduct business in plain view without fear of discovery. When a team was negotiating with a particular player, the team would notify Brunell, and in turn, he would warn the other seven clubs not to interfere. Only nine people knew about and had access to the cipher. Because of his administrative responsibilities with the Pittsburgh team, John Tener was one of these.[10]

When the Players League folded after a single season, Hanlon returned to the National League, and continued the career that would eventually find him in the Hall of Fame. For his part, Tener returned to the Pittsburgh area and resumed his business career. He was named the cashier for the First National Bank of Charleroi, an executive position, eventually rising to president of the bank. In addition, he organized the Charleroi Savings and Trust Company and the second Mercantile Bridge Company. Throughout this time, he remained active in the local baseball scene as a player, manager, or sponsor of local amateur teams.[11] In 1891, with the sponsorship of the Allegheny Athletic Association, he sought to have his amateur status restored so that he might play in an anticipated high-level amateur league, including teams from Detroit, Cleveland, Chicago, Jersey City, New York, and Boston. Commenting on the application, Tener said, "I don't see why the authorities should hesitate in reinstating me, and I believe they will when the facts of the case are made known to them."[12] They did not. A spokesman for the governing body of the sport put it succinctly: "You can set it down as a fact that the Amateur Athletic Union will never reinstate a man who has made a living out of baseball . . . If the Allegheny Athletic Association expects to win the amateur baseball championship through the medium of the reinstatement of professional baseball players, they are liable to come in contact with several large and frosty consignments of disappointments."[13]

During this time, Tener also began to develop an interest in elective office.

Two steppingstones advanced that cause. The first was the bridge company. A predecessor firm of the same name had been formed in 1903 to build a bridge across the Monongahela River, joining the suburbs of Charleroi and Monessen, but the venture had failed. At that point, Tener and some colleagues had stepped in, reconstituted the company, overcome challenges from weather and high water, and successfully built the bridge, which opened in 1907. Tener served as president of the bridge company and, upon completion of the work, as vice president of the eight-mile-long street railway company that would use the bridge to provide a public transit connection between the two communities. His brother George Jr., a successful entrepreneur in his own right, also served on the railway board. This was seen locally as a highly significant civic improvement.[14]

Also in 1907, John Tener was elected as the national Grand Exalted Ruler of the Protective Order of Elks, AKA the Elks Club. Tener had previously served the group as Grand Treasurer. This provided him with renewed national visibility as well as a platform for traveling around Pennsylvania and the remainder of the country and a natural and well-organized constituency.[15] And an adoring constituency it appears to have been. In the words of one observer, "Mr. Tener is a splendid type of manhood, a man whose shoulders seem broad enough to bear the responsibilities that are placed upon them. He is over six feet tall and excellently proportioned."[16] Lest the point be lost on those observers, soon-to-be-president "Bill" Taft sent a telegram to one such Elks gathering saying that if Tener were elected to Congress, Taft would appoint him as a cabinet secretary."[17]

In 1908, Tener defeated the incumbent Republican Congressman Ernest F. Acheson for the party's nomination in the first contest under Pennsylvania's then-new primary election process, which, among other things, required voters to declare a party identity. Though Tener was a popular candidate and the outcome was clear, the process came under

scrutiny with claims that some Democrats had voted in the GOP bal-
loting to benefit Tener while some Prohibitionists had crossed over to
benefit Acheson.[18] In the general election, Reverend Frank Fish, the
Prohibitionist candidate for the congressional seat, claimed that early
in the year the state's liquor interests had put up $100,000 to assure
Tener's nomination. This was likely occasioned by an open letter Tener
had posted in March indicating that as a congressman he would not seek
to impose restrictions on alcohol sales since that was a matter of state,
not federal, policy and that he was an advocate for what was termed
local option. Tener was quick to respond to Fish's allegation. "My lifelong
respect for his vocation, that of minister of the gospel," he said, "led me
to conclude that he would very soon at least attempt to ascertain the
truth. His failure to do so is evidence of either a willful determination
to deceive the voters or his reliance upon a source of information that is
self-interested, vindictive and unworthy of confidence." Tener had clearly
learned the political art of indirect insult. His official reports showed that
he had spent some $14,000 in obtaining the nomination and $850 in the
general election—far less than Fish had claimed but regarded at the time
as excessive nonetheless.[19]

Whether or not the claim was sour grapes on the part of a defeated
opponent, in December 1908, the *Washington Observer* newspaper,
owned by defeated rival Ernest Acheson, suggested that Tener's interest
in serving in Congress was merely a waypoint toward a larger ambition.

> John K. Tener is a full-fledged candidate for governor . . . Tener's
> intimate friends say that he has no taste for congressional duties
> and only sought that office as a steppingstone to something
> higher. They allege that he did not want to run for congress, but
> that the governorship appeals to him."[20]

Whatever his motive, Acheson was very close to the mark.

THE TARIFF TICK-TOCK

THE TIME HAS come to explain what this story is really all about.

Yes, this is a story about a baseball game, but it is also a story about political gamesmanship. Indeed, the argument here is that the two were inseparable and that the "game" was played to serve the purposes of the chief gamesman. One cannot understand why a group of congressmen, generally not the most athletic (or even fit) of men, suddenly decided for the very first time to stand up opposing teams and humiliate themselves in a public display of something approximating the national pastime on a hot July afternoon in 1909 without first taking into account the struggle then taking place on Capitol Hill, and especially in the U.S. House of Representatives. It was a struggle that contained all the basics of a sordid political drama: unnumbered special interests, sectionalism, ideological clashes, an abundance of devilish details to fight over, uncertain outcomes, distrust, resentment, boredom, personal bitterness, intense partisanship, cleverness, and cynicism; all presided over by a tyrannical leader with an agenda. Oh, and I almost forgot. It was also a story about money. A great deal of money. Enough money literally to reshape the entire economy *and* to run the federal government.

The genesis of the first congressional baseball game began long before the Sixty-First Congress, that of 1909-1910, ever convened. To appreciate the significance of the game itself and the role it was meant to play, we need to begin with that background.

To be sure, the members of Congress are always fighting about something. With some justification, they seem to think it's the reason the

American people have sent them there. Some of these battles are truly mundane, the legislative equivalent of busywork, while others are fundamental. And as difficult as it may be for us today to appreciate the fact, in 1909, the battle over the nation's policy on tariffs, the very issue that had brought together the delegation that attended the Orioles-Royals baseball game and that was so much discussed during their visit, was one that fell into the latter category.

Tariffs, or import duties, are taxes that a national government imposes on foreign goods that are sold into its domestic markets. The idea of tariffs is to help domestic industries compete with foreign manufacturers who might be able to produce goods more cheaply for one reason or another. They are an alternative to providing subsidies. The higher the tariff on the imported version of any given product, the greater the protection its domestic competition is afforded. But that protection comes at a cost. Higher tariffs translate into higher prices for consumers. At the same time, higher tariffs also bring more money into the government's coffers, supporting whatever programs or services it might choose to provide. In effect, then, tariffs must serve three overlapping but competitive interests: those of the nation's economy, the nation's people, and the nation's government.

As topics go, tariffs can be as boring as it gets. Traditionally, tariffs have been among the most arcane and complicated matters that ever come before Congress, which was surely the case in 1909. Think about it this way. If you were to create a piece of legislation that was vitally important and a piece of legislation that ran for hundreds and hundreds of pages of small print that detailed the specific and disparate impact of the proposed law on every single segment of the economy and every company and every product and that, as a result, created thousands of winners and losers depending on the specific language of each element of the law, why, you couldn't do better than to write a new tariff bill. Then, throw in a new tax on the income of corporations and a new constitutional amendment that would allow the government to tax the incomes of individual citizens as well. Then, just for good measure, set some rules that will all but prohibit debate on the bill and force a vote, all the while preventing any other business from moving through Congress until things come out your way. And while you're at it, why not dress up the first draft of your bill so it looks like it will aggressively *reduce* tariffs and free up international trade, which would, in turn, lower prices on all of these imported goods? But know with certainty that your friends over in the Senate will fix that for you and that the version that eventually comes back for passage will do nothing of the sort. Talk about playing hardball.

If your name was Joseph Gurney Cannon, "Uncle Joe," and you were the all-powerful Speaker of the U.S. House of Representatives in 1909, that was precisely your game.

In service to the public interest, we can skip over the details of the legislation and the tariffs themselves. Whew! But if our goal is to understand the dynamic that led to the playing of CBG1, there is no escaping the politics of the issue. For that, let's rely on what journalists call "the tick-tock" of the matter, the chronological order of events leading to and following from the playing of the game.

Two hundred or so years ago, when the country was small and less economically developed and when the federal government was very limited in its size and scope, the United States adopted a highly protectionist system of tariffs. Those tax revenues were the main source of money for funding the government, and they were more or less sufficient for that purpose. But when the Civil War came along, the Union needed vast new flows of cash, cash that it raised through taxes on real estate, inheritances, whiskey, other business activities, and, yes, individual incomes. In 1881, the Supreme Court upheld these new taxes, including the income tax, as being constitutional, but in a later test, *Pollock v. Farmers' Loan & Trust Company*, in 1895, the Court reversed itself, declaring that the income tax in particular was unconstitutional.[1] As you can imagine, that created something of a cash flow problem for the government, to which Congress responded in 1897 by passing the highly protectionist Dingley Tariff Act. But they did too good a job of it. Dingley raised more income than the government needed in order to operate. That set up a massive struggle among traditional Republicans who wanted to maintain the tariffs to protect their favored industries, populist Democrats led by William Jennings Bryan, who wanted to shrink the tariffs way back to serve the interests of primarily rural families, and a new third force, progressive Republicans led by Theodore Roosevelt, who wanted to end the use of tariffs to protect the massive corporate trusts that had come to dominate large sectors of the economy while replacing and even growing the resultant lost revenue so that they could build a new structure of regulatory agencies to govern economic activity. All of this came to a head in 1909.

Anticipating that the issue would dominate the coming Sixty-First Congress in 1908, the Republican leadership, which controlled the White House and both houses of Congress, took two important steps. First, in Congress, Speaker Joseph Cannon pushed the Ways and Means Committee to begin work on new tariff legislation. Ways and Means was chaired by Sereno Payne of New York, whom we have already met. Payne, like Cannon, was a protectionist from the GOP establishment, and like Cannon, he was aware of the pressure for reform. The political challenge the pair faced, then, was how they might produce so-called tariff reform that was, in fact, scarcely a reform at all. The solution they settled on was a cynical power play.

For many months in 1908, Payne led his committee in researching the tariff rates and drafting new tariff legislation with many reductions in the levies, though the plan was that this bill would not be brought out of the committee until the beginning of the new Congress the following year. The committee produced 953 pages of related court decisions and other documents, and on November 10, immediately following the presidential (and congressional) election, it began a set of hearings that were held almost daily until Christmas, during which several hundred witnesses presented testimony.[2] All of this activity created the appearance of a genuine move toward reform, but without locking that outcome into place.

Meanwhile, in their platform for the 1908 presidential election, without taking any position on specific tariffs or reform, the Republicans committed the new president, if elected, to calling a special session of Congress to address the issue.[3] This mollified the Roosevelt faction, and the party candidate, Taft, who was openly sympathetic to tariff reform, indicated that he would follow through on the party's commitment. The incoming president recognized that Speaker Cannon would be an impediment to passing such reforms, and his first impulse was to organize the reform faction of his party in Congress to overthrow the Speaker and replace him with one of their number to ease the way. Unfortunately for Taft, when he surveyed the field, he found that there were no more than thirty votes for this act of rebellion, and he abandoned the effort.[4] On March 15, Taft convened the special session of Congress that had been promised in the 1908 platform.

Though the president had given up on deposing Speaker Cannon, the band of Republican insurgents still had one hand to play.

At the beginning of each session of Congress, the House votes on the general rules that will govern debate in the weeks ahead. As the 1909 session opened, the Republican insurgents, which is to say, the progressives in the House, joined with the Democrats to challenge the proposed rules backed by the Speaker. This led to a bitter and sometimes quite personal daylong parliamentary struggle that was eventually resolved when Representative John J. Fitzgerald of New York, a Democrat acting in clear concert with the other side, introduced a compromise that was immediately accepted by Speaker Cannon and adopted by the majority of Republicans augmented by some two dozen of the more conservative Democrats. This was the action that led to Fitzgerald being labeled an outcast among the Democrats. Cannon then named Mr. Fitzgerald to the Rules Committee as an obvious reward and appointed another Democratic rebel, Robert Broussard of Louisiana, a known protectionist, to Ways and Means. Broussard may have been appointed to ensure that any protectionist tariff legislation that might eventually be issued from the committee could be claimed as bipartisan. The Democrats howled in protest in much the same way, and over the very same issue, which led Republicans to object loudly in 2021 when then-Speaker Nancy Pelosi named two Republicans of her own choosing to the committee investigating the January 6 disruption in the Capitol Building.

And then it got personal between the Speaker and Champ Clark, the Minority Leader. As reported in the Louisville *Courier-Journal*,

> The Speaker called on the President early in the morning [of March 16], and when he was leaving the executive offices made this answer to a question as to the fight in the House yesterday:
> "The amendments to the rules have greatly improved them. All this stuff about the Speaker being a czar is the purest tommyrot. There has never been a time when the majority could not control the House. What they wanted to do was to make

a committee of fifteen czars, dominated by Champ Clark and [progressive Republican and Taft foe Wisconsin Senator Robert] LaFollette. That is also tommyrot. LaFollette is a fake."

When Representative Champ Clark . . . was told what the Speaker had said, he answered briefly:

"Uncle Joe [Cannon] has paresis."[5]

Paresis refers to an inflammation of the brain in late-stage syphilis that causes progressive dementia. It seems unlikely this was meant as a compliment.

It was in that context, then, that the House turned to its first, and as matters developed, nearly its only item of substantive business, the aforementioned tariff bill. Here, in a highly abbreviated form, is how things went.

DATE	DAY	ACTION
MAR 15	001	President Taft convenes the Special Session.
MAR 16	002	Taft sends a message explaining that the session has been called "to give immediate consideration to the Dingley Tariff Act."
MAR 17	003	Payne introduces the bill Ways and Means had drafted in 1908; the bill is referred to Ways and Means for consideration.
MAR 18	004	Ways and Means reports the bill to the House with a favorable recommendation.[6]
MAR 19	005	Debate on the bill opens under a rule that permits amendments only by the Ways and Means Committee and not from the floor.
MAR 20	006	
MAR 21	007	
MAR 22	008	
MAR 23	009	
MAR 24	010	

DATE	DAY	ACTION
MAR 25	011	
MAR 26	012	
MAR 27	013	
MAR 28	014	
MAR 29	015	
MAR 30	016	
MAR 31	017	
APR 1	018	
APR 2	019	
APR 3	020	
APR 4	021	
APR 5	022	
APR 6	023	
APR 7	024	
APR 8	025	
APR 9	026	The House passes the Payne Tariff Act by a vote of 217-161; refers the bill to the Senate.

At this point, we need to interrupt the compelling pace of congressional action to introduce Senator Nelson Aldrich of Rhode Island, a staunch protectionist in his own right who has been waiting in the wings to play his assigned role. Senator Nelson chairs the Finance Committee, the Senate's functional equivalent of Ways and Means in the House. This, in case you might miss it, is where the game takes a turn.

DATE	DAY	ACTION
APR 9		Senator Nelson introduces the Payne Tariff Act; the bill is referred to the Finance Committee.

DATE	DAY	ACTION
APR 10	027	
APR 11	028	
APR 12	029	The Finance Committee reports the bill back to the Senate.
APR 13	030	
APR 14	031	
APR 15	032	
APR 16	033	
APR 17	034	
APR 18	035	
APR 19	036	Over the next eleven weeks, the Senate will debate the Payne Tariff Act. Meanwhile, in the House of Representatives . . .
APR 20	037	
APR 21	038	
APR 22	039	
APR 23	040	
APR 24	041	
APR 25	042	
APR 26	043	
APR 27	044	
APR 28	045	
APR 29	046	
APR 30	047	
MAY 1	048	
MAY 2	049	
MAY 3	050	
MAY 4	051	
MAY 5	052	
MAY 6	053	
MAY 7	054	
MAY 8	055	
MAY 9	056	
MAY 10	057	

DATE	DAY	ACTION
MAY 11	058	
MAY 12	059	
MAY 13	060	
MAY 14	061	
MAY 15	062	
MAY 16	063	
MAY 17	064	
MAY 18	065	
MAY 19	066	
MAY 20	067	
MAY 21	068	
MAY 22	069	
MAY 23	070	
MAY 24	071	
MAY 25	072	
MAY 26	073	
MAY 27	074	
MAY 28	075	
MAY 29	076	
MAY 30	077	
MAY 31	078	

If it appears at this point as if nothing is happening in the House, that is precisely correct. In fact, it is extremely correct, for the Speaker of the House has done a very unusual thing. *Essentially, he has shut down the House.*

All legislative action in the House is typically channeled through a large number of committees, each with a specialized jurisdiction. In the Sixtieth Congress (1907-1908), for example, there were sixty-odd such committees, a typical number for the era. For most of the initial (1909) session of the Sixty-First Congress, there were but five.[7] Three of these comprised a literal handful of members who were charged with such routine matters as determining the mileage traveled by Members in coming to Washington from their home districts and making sure Members were paid. One, somewhat larger, was the Rules Committee, chaired by the Speaker's protectionist colleague, John Dalzell, but including the Speaker as a member, wherein resided control over the debate on the House floor and the power of appointment of members of both parties to all the other committees, and Ways and Means, chaired by Mr. Payne, which had jurisdiction over both the tariff and any tax legislation. *No other committees were named*, which had the effect of shutting down all other legislative activity. Nothing else could move, nor would it, Cannon made clear, until the final passage of both items and, specifically, the tariff bill. And that's where things stood as May turned to June.

DATE	DAY	ACTION
JUN 1	079	
JUN 2	080	
JUN 3	081	
JUN 4	082	
JUN 5	083	
JUN 6	084	
JUN 7	085	
JUN 8	086	
JUN 9	087	
JUN 10	088	
JUN 11	089	
JUN 12	090	
JUN 13	091	
JUN 14	092	
JUN 15	093	
JUN 16	094	As floor debate on the Tariff Act continues in the Senate, and as members of the House twiddle their thumbs, President Taft drops the other shoe with a message calling for passage of what would be the Sixteenth Amendment to the Constitution, allowing for the imposition of a personal income tax.
JUN 17	095	

DATE	DAY	ACTION
JUN 18	096	
JUN 19	097	
JUN 20	098	
JUN 21	099	
JUN 22	100	It is on this day, one hundred days into the session, that John Tener telephones Ned Hanlon to arrange the congressional and lobbyist delegation's visit to Baltimore.
JUN 23	101	Payne, Tener, and the others attend the baseball game in Baltimore; talk turns to the tariff bill
JUN 24	102	
JUN 25	103	
JUN 26	104	
JUN 27	105	
JUN 28	106	Senator Aldrich introduces S. J. R. (Senate Joint Resolution) 40, the income tax amendment, in the Senate; the measure is also conveyed to the House.
JUN 29	107	
JUN 30	108	

Let's intervene briefly in the narrative here to make clear what is happening. The House has passed and sent to the Senate a version of the tariff bill that looks to all the world like a serious effort at reform, which is to say, tariff reduction. No reform advocates in the House had any opportunity to amend the bill before passage, but on balance, it seems to move in their direction. The Senate has been debating the bill on the floor for more than two months, adding hundreds of amendments. This is worrisome for the reformers, but they are reassured somewhat by the fact that one of these amendments has added to the bill the corporate income tax, which they find both philosophically pleasing and financially useful because it has the potential to offset some of the revenues lost to tariff reductions at the expense of the industrial and financial trusts they so despise. And now, the president has called for additional reinforcement in the form of an income tax, which Senator Aldrich has brought forward and which Speaker Cannon and the other protectionists in the House have endorsed. For their part, much as the protectionists and their allies in both houses dislike the income tax, they are happy to get behind it for one simple reason: They are confident that when the amendment goes to the states, it will fail of ratification. In other words, their calculus is that they can afford to support the amendment as a signal to the reformers that tariff reform really is coming because (a) they believe the tax amendment will never take effect, and (b) they know they have the power and the votes to pass the fully protectionist amended tariff bill that Senator Aldrich is preparing to send them.

DATE	DAY	ACTION
JUL 1	109	
JUL 2	110	
JUL 3	111	
JUL 4	112	
JUL 5	113	
JUL 6	114	
JUL 7	115	
JUL 8	116	The Senate passes what is now known as the Payne-Aldrich Tariff Act with 847 amendments, including the new 2 percent tax on the incomes of corporations, by a vote of 45-34, with 13 Senators not voting. Put another way, the legislation has passed but has failed to achieve a majority vote. Nevertheless, the tariff bill as amended, is returned to the House for a vote.
JUL 9	117	After enduring a wait of three months, during which it was unable to conduct any business, the House votes to reject the Senate version of the bill. To this point, all of the action has taken place more or less in public view, but that is about to change. The House and the Senate both agree to send their respective versions of the bill to a conference committee to work out the differences.

House consideration of the tariff bill has now entered the endgame, with the conference committee completely under the control of Speaker Cannon, Chairman Payne, and Chairman Aldrich. Everyone has seen the 847 Senate amendments, and the outcome cannot be in doubt. The power centers have held, and the false promise of meaningful tariff reductions, of so-called free trade, has been revealed as a sham. The tick-tock continues.

DATE	DAY	ACTION
JUL 10	118	The first news report is published announcing the pending congressional baseball game.
JUL 11	119	
JUL 12	120	Two weeks after its introduction, the Sixteenth Amendment passes both houses of Congress and is sent to the states for ratification, which requires the concurrence of three-quarters of the state legislatures.
JUL 13	121	
JUL 14	122	
JUL 15	123	While the Payne-Aldrich bill is in the conference committee, President Taft proposes his own amendments.

Now, let's add one more consideration. On June 20, 1909, as summer officially began, daytime high temperatures in Washington, which had been mostly in the sixties and seventies for weeks, spiked suddenly. The highs from June 20 through the end of the month were 90, 91, 90, 92, 90, 93, 94, 93, 92, 89, 88. The trend continued in July: 90, 88, 86, and after a few more moderate days, went right back up. Rainfall through the period was a bit below average, but the humidity, though not included in the Weather Service database, was almost surely high—typically in the range of 80-95 percent.[8] It is not a myth that Washington was literally built on a swamp. While it is true that Willis Carrier invented mechanical refrigeration (air conditioning) in 1902 and the organizers of the St. Louis World's Fair used such a system to cool the Missouri State Building in 1904, it was not until 1935 that Congress appropriated funds for installing central refrigeration equipment to cool its various buildings.[9]

It was inescapably hot and probably quite humid.

So, let us consider the situation in the House of Representatives in the middle of July 1909. Members are called to a special session in March, requiring them to travel to Washington earlier than they may have anticipated. Then, they are presented with a highly complex tariff bill, which, they are told, is a first step toward the reform that is being widely promoted, but they are given no opportunity to amend it before passage. Regardless, the bill passes in early April and goes to the Senate where, they can see, it is subjected to extensive debate and literally hundreds of amendments. In the meantime, in mid-June, the President calls for a constitutional amendment to permit the levying of an income tax, and within days, on July 12, Senate Joint Resolution 40, the income tax amendment, passes both houses. In early July, the much-revised Senate tariff bill is rejected and sent to conference for reconciliation. But that's it. And everyone understands what is about to happen.

At that point, then, the *only* thing the Representatives have accomplished over four months in Washington is a move to tax the incomes of their constituents. There are no policy committees in place other than Ways and Means, so there is no other legislation moving anywhere in the House, and hence, there is very little to do other than wait for the conference committee to report back the tariff legislation in its final form. Yet they must remain in town during a typically uncomfortable Washington summer, many of them long separated from home and family in an era before commercial aviation. Tempers must flare; the pressure must build. That is only human, and these are politicians, men (and they were all men at that time) with large egos, constituents setting expectations, lobbyists waiting to lobby and to lavish them with campaign contributions to influence legislation that does not exist and cannot be created, and prospective electoral opponents rubbing their hands in glee and eager anticipation. Something has to give. Some relief from the pressure must be found.

Enter the congressional baseball game.

Figure 4. Just what the doctor ordered?

MISTER TENER GOES TO WASHINGTON

INTO THE MIDDLE of this budding political melee stepped John Kinley Tener. Since he had last visited the nation's capital in 1889 when he was pitching for the White Stockings against the Washington Nationals, Tener made a post-election reconnaissance visit of sorts on December 10, 1908. And he was treated upon his arrival as something of a celebrity. As the magazine *Sporting Life* put it succinctly, "One touch of base ball makes the whole world kin."

Tener was greeted by John Williams, Clerk of the House, who introduced him to the Speaker, "Uncle Joe" Cannon, Vice President-elect James Sherman, Congressman John Dalzell, who served as Chairman of the powerful Committee on Rules, which, as we have seen, determined what items of business would be brought to the floor of the House and under what structure each would be debated, and others. When he mentioned that he had known Supreme Court Associate Justice Moody during his early years at Haverhill, Williams escorted him over to the Supreme Court chamber, which was still located in the Capitol Building in those days. Tener and Williams were standing along a corridor rope line to watch the justices return from lunch when Moody spotted his old friend. He walked over to shake hands, and the pair walked off and exchanged reminiscences of batting averages, sensational plays, and pitching records while Moody's colleagues on the bench were kept waiting.[1]

When the Sixty-First Congress opened in March 1909, Tener was the ultimate backbencher. He was a first-term congressman who, like all but a select few of his colleagues, had, for the moment, no committee assignments. He had, as Acheson had claimed, no apparent interest in pursuing a second term. During 1909, he sponsored nineteen bills, seventeen of them for the purpose of increasing the pension of one or another of his constituents and two for the relief of individuals under more general legislation.[2] He demonstrated no interest in specific policies, though, near the end of the session, when Speaker Cannon finally named members to the standing committees of the House, he was given a seat on the Committee on Rivers and Harbors, probably because of his recent experience in leading the construction of a major bridge. During his two years on Capitol Hill, the House took two hundred roll call votes. Tener missed one hundred twenty-four of those, or sixty-two percent. That compares against the average for all members with whom he served of twenty-seven percent of votes missed. On the major issue of the first session, the tariff, however, Tener's was a reliable party-line vote. The only time he split with the leadership was to support an amendment placing petroleum on the free trade list rather than assigning a duty—understandable given Pennsylvania's interest in the petroleum industry.[3] It is fair to say that, but for his celebrity status among some members, John Tener did not fit the profile of an influential member of Congress. And by the end of his term, his attention was all but fully focused on his pursuit of the governorship of his state.

This, then, is the John Tener, who is widely credited with conceiving, organizing, and successfully bringing about the first congressional baseball game.[4]

That argument is certainly plausible. Tener did come to Congress with a bit of fame as a one-time major league baseball player, and he was clearly a convivial sort who made friends easily and then kept them. He was experienced in arranging complex enterprises. His longtime friendship with Baltimore Orioles president Ned Hanlon undoubtedly came into play in the June road trip. And it is likely that one of the others on that trip, Judge J.B. Fisher, was a prior acquaintance. Fisher had served as a member of the Exalted Board of Grand Trustees, the national board of directors of the Elks organization, at roughly the same time that Tener was among the group's top officers. There is no question that he played some role in bringing CBG1 into reality. But there are other claimants to originating the idea for the matchup, as well as questions about the interpretation of events.

One possibility is that the game was a product of the athletic version of spontaneous combustion—that it just happened. A detailed account in the *Cincinnati Enquirer*, for instance, noted that "the game had been brewing for weeks, and the members of the House were keyed up to a high pitch of enthusiasm." And even as the teams organized themselves with care, by game time, no agreement had been reached as to who might serve as umpire. Among the names suggested by Republicans—and rejected by Democrats as unfairly partisan or otherwise unworthy—were Vice President Sherman; Speaker Cannon; Henry Bingham, Republican of Pennsylvania, the longest continuously serving congressman, who had held his seat since 1879 and was known as the Father of the House; and Nehemiah Day Sperry, Republican of Connecticut, the oldest member of the body. A last-minute compromise was reached, with Jim O'Day [misidentified in some contemporaneous news accounts], the groundskeeper of the ballpark where the game was to be played, chosen to call balls and strikes and the Reverend Father James Reynolds, a Catholic priest from Red Bank, New Jersey, assigned to referee the basepaths.[5]

Alternatively, the game may have been proposed by the Democrats. That, at least, was the claim in a *Washington Post* pregame article, which noted that the minority delegation [the Democrats] "are tired of the drubbing which their Republican brethren have administered to them on the floor of the House, and have challenged their opponents to a tryout on the diamond." Specifically, John Nance "Cactus Jack" Garner of Texas reportedly hurled the dare at Tener, who smiled and replied that he would happily get together a team. According to this July 10 report, Garner planned to captain a team that included congressmen James McDermott (Illinois), Ollie James (Kentucky), Eugene Kinkead and William Hughes (both of New Jersey), Finis Garrett (Tennessee), Daniel Driscoll (New York), Joseph O'Connell (Massachusetts), and John McHenry (Pennsylvania), while Tener's GOP roster would include John Morehead (North Carolina), Frank Lowden and William McKinley (both of Illinois), James Burke (Pennsylvania), Politte Elvins (Missouri), Edward Vreeland and William Bennett (both of New York), and Victor Murdock (Kansas).[6] In the end, the Democrats' gameday lineup included all of those Garner listed except for McHenry and Garner himself. Of those proposed by Tener, however, only he and Burke eventually played in the game, while Vreeland would have done so but for an injury. At least on the surface, then, this did not give the appearance of a well-plotted Tener initiative.

There was, as well, another Republican claimant to the founding. Mr. Vreeland of New York, an influential member of the majority who had been on the original roster for the earlier visit to Baltimore and was in line to chair the Committee on Banking when it was eventually constituted, laid claim to that title and the captaincy of the GOP squad as well. Unfortunately, as we will see, he was not able to compete in the actual contest.[7]

But let us consider another, less obvious, point of origin, one that derives from the broader context in which the game was played.

Consider: John Tener came to Congress as a well-known, personable, and highly ambitious man recognized for his finance-related skill set. But he was also the most junior of congressmen and a short-timer from the outset, distracted and disengaged from the legislative responsibilities of his new position. He had baseball chops and baseball connections, but even less than a week before CBG1 would eventually be played, he had not recruited more than one or two prospective teammates. One of those, Mr. Vreeland, was actually a co-claimant to having conceived the game, and John Garner, the Democrat, was farther along in identifying potential players. Tener was not a central figure in any of the backroom dealing or public debate relating to the primary issue of the day—and not coincidentally, the source of much of the friction in the House—the tariff bill.

Consider: By late June, the dissatisfaction with Speaker Cannon, and through him with Majority Leader Payne, was substantial and increasing. Likely, the confidence of the more reform-minded Republicans that the final form of the tariff bill would retain the reductions in duties they had voted for was on the wane. To address that, President Taft, who badly wanted a tariff bill—*any* tariff bill—had just proposed the income tax amendment, something that the congressional leadership, probably among many others, had known to expect. Aldrich would introduce it in Congress just days after the Baltimore trip. What better time for a strategy session to keep the momentum going through the summer? But might not such a skull session, including Payne's protectionist allies, the recently-retired GOP whip who still knew how to garner votes in the caucus, a leading protectionist lobbyist or two, and perhaps even a potential Democratic swing voter who had already cut one deal in the drafting process, best be held away from the Capitol? Perhaps one of the original planners, Mr. Vreeland, and/or Mr. Payne, also a fan of the game, had put some pieces together and come up with a short visit up the road to an Orioles game as a perfect opportunity for a candid back-stage conversation. That, at least, was the view of *The Washington Post*, which characterized the traveling party as "headed by Sereno E. Payne."[8] And there was even a perfect resource person available to arrange such a visit—freshman Representative John K. Tener.

Consider: The Baltimore travelers chose to go by automobile. It is possible that in this they were influenced by the publicity associated with the first transcontinental automobile race across North America; the winning vehicle, a Ford, arrived at the finish line in Seattle that very same day, June 23, 1909. The race, promoted as a test of the durability of the automobile, had attracted considerable publicity.[9] How about a short road trip of their own? But there were surely easier and more convenient ways to make the trip. As just one example, the Washington, Baltimore & Annapolis Electric Railway operated a daily schedule of nonstop cars that departed Washington from the White House Station at Fifteenth and H Streets, NE, at the time, an easy streetcar or taxi connection from the group's jumping off point at the Willard Hotel (or from the Capitol), every half hour between six in the morning and midnight, arriving at Terminal Station (Park Avenue and Liberty Street near Lexington) in central Baltimore about ten blocks from the Belvedere Hotel an hour and a quarter later, returning on a comparable schedule.[10] The difference? Travel using the railway, while convenient and more reliable, was also much more public. Travel by auto, on the other hand, allowed for private conversation of precisely the type one might desire when discussing political strategy.

Consider: Even the public focus of the preliminary trip to Baltimore was heavily centered on the ongoing dispute over the tariff, which by then had been wending its way through the Senate for more than two months. While at the game, every participant was asked to comment on the legislation, and all but one, Mr. Byrns, the lone Democrat, parroted

Washington, Baltimore and Annapolis Electric Railway Co.

THE ELECTRIC LINE

RATES OF FARE.

	ONE WAY	ROUND TRIP
Baltimore-Washington	$ .75	$1.25
Baltimore-Annapolis	.60	1.00
Washington-Annapolis	.75	1.25

TICKETS GOOD UNTIL USED.

COMMUTATION AND PARTY RATES
WILL BE FURNISHED ON APPLICATION.

TICKET OFFICES.

WASHINGTON—Fourteenth St. and New York
Ave. Northwest and White House Station, Fif-
teenth and H Sts. Northeast.
BALTIMORE—Terminal Station, Park Ave. and
Liberty St., between Fayette and Lexington
Sts. and Albaugh's, 109 N. Charles St.
ANNAPOLIS—West St. Station, Maryland Hotel,
Carvel Hall, Green's Drug Store, W. H.
Moss, opp. Governor's Mansion, and U. S.
Naval Academy P. O. (for Naval officers only.)

BUY TICKETS FROM AGENTS.   NONE SOLD ON CARS.

BAGGAGE CHECKED

Direct connections with city cars in Washington with free transfers to all points in
the District of Columbia on the the lines of
the Washington Railway and Electric Co. The
only line between Baltimore and Annapolis whose
cars reach the centers of both cities, connect in
Baltimore with all principal street car lines and reach
the gate of the famous United States Naval
Academy at Annapolis.

GENERAL OFFICES
TERMINAL STATION BUILDING
PARK AVE. AND LIBERTY ST.
BET. FAYETTE & LEXINGTON STS.
BALTIMORE, MD.

IN EFFECT APRIL 1, 1909.

WASHINGTON BALTIMORE & ANNAPOLIS ELECTRIC RY.

FAST ELECTRIC CARS
THE GREATEST DOUBLE TRACK INTERURBAN ELECTRIC LINE
IN THE WORLD.

These time tables supersede all others previously issued
and are subject to change and correction without notice.
The Company will not be responsible for consequences
arising from errors in these printed schedules.

For tickets and information, apply at City Ticket Offices
or address General Passenger Agent, Baltimore, Md.

DAILY

BALTIMORE AND ANNAPOLIS

Cars leave Baltimore from Terminal Station, Park Ave. and Liberty
St., near Lexington. The Annapolis time indicates West St. Station,
but all cars leave U. S. Naval Academy ten minutes earlier and Governor's Mansion seven minutes earlier and arrive at these points five
and three minutes later respectively than arriving time here given.

Leave Baltimore.	Arrive Annapolis.	Leave Baltimore.	Arrive Baltimore.
6.45 A. M.	7.45 A. M.	5.30 A. M.	6.30 A. M.
7.45	8.45	6.30	7.30
8.45	9.45	7.30	8.30
9.45	10.45	8.30	9.30
10.45	11.45	9.30	10.30
11.45	11.45 P. M.	10.30	11.30
12.45 P. M.	1.45	11.30	12.30 P. M.
1.45	2.45	12.30 P. M.	1.30
2.45	3.45	1.30	2.30
3.45	4.45	2.30	3.30
4.45	5.45	3.30	4.30
5.45	6.45	4.30	5.30
6.15	7.30	5.30	6.30
6.45	7.45	6.30	7.30
7.45	8.45	7.45	8.45
8.30	9.30	8.30	9.30
9.45	10.45	10.30	11.30
11.55	12.55		

EXPLANATION OF SIGNS: *Limited. n Local Baltimore to
Naval Academy Jct. to discharge passengers only. s Transfer at
Naval Academy Jct. t Will stop on signal at Camp Parole and
Millersville to receive through passengers for Baltimore and Naval
Academy Jct. n Will stop on signal at High Bridge to receive
through passengers for Baltimore and Naval Academy Jct.

WASHINGTON AND ANNAPOLIS

(REQUIRING CHANGE AT NAVAL ACADEMY JUNCTION.)

Cars leave Washington from White House Station, 13th and B
Sts. N. E. The Annapolis line indicates West St. Station, but all
cars leave U. S. Naval Academy ten minutes earlier, and Governor's
Mansion seven minutes earlier and arrive at these points five and
three minutes later respectively than arriving time here given.

Leave Washington.	Arrive Annapolis.	Leave Annapolis.	Arrive Washington.
6.30 A. M.	7.45 A. M.	5.30 A. M.	6.45 A. M.
7.30	8.45	6.30	7.45
8.30	9.45	7.30	8.45
9.30	10.45	8.30	9.45
10.30	11.45	9.30	10.45
11.30	12.45 P. M.	10.30	11.45
12.30 P. M.	1.45	11.30	12.45 P. M.
1.30	2.45	12.30 P. M.	1.45
2.30	3.45	1.30	2.45
3.30	4.45	2.30	3.45
4.30	5.45	3.30	4.45
5.30	6.45	4.30	5.45
6.30	7.45	5.30	6.45
7.30	8.45	6.30	7.45
8.30	9.30	7.45	8.45
9.30	10.45	8.30	9.45
11.46	12.55 A. M.	10.30	11.45

EXPLANATION OF SIGNS: *Limited. t Will stop on signal
at Camp Parole and Millersville to receive through passengers for
Naval Academy Jct. and Washington. s Will stop on signal at
Camp Parole to receive through passengers for Naval Academy Jct.
and Washington.

DAILY
WASHINGTON AND BALTIMORE. LIMITED CARS.

Leave Baltimore.	Arrive Washington.	Leave Washington.	Arrive Baltimore.
* 6.00 A. M.	7.10 A. M.	6.00 A. M.	7.15 A. M.
6.30	7.45	6.35	7.45
* 7.30	8.30	7.30	8.45
7.30	8.45	* 8.00	9.30
* 8.00	9.10	8.30	9.45
8.30	9.45	9.30	10.45
* 9.00	10.10	*10.00	11.10
9.30	10.45	10.30	11.45
*10.00	11.10	11.30	12.45 P. M.
10.30	11.45	*12.00 Noon	1.30
11.30	12.45 P. M.	12.30 P. M.	1.45
*12.00 Noon	1.10	1.30	2.45
12.30 P. M.	1.45	*2.00	3.10
1.30	2.45	2.30	3.45
*2.00	3.10	3.30	4.45
2.30	3.45	*4.00	5.30
3.30	4.45	4.30	5.45
*4.00	5.10	5.30	6.30
4.30	5.45	*6.00	7.10
5.30	6.45	6.30	7.45
6.30	7.45	7.30	8.45
7.30	8.45	8.30	9.45
8.30n	9.45	9.30	10.45
9.30	10.45	10.30	11.45
10.30	11.45	11.45	1.03 A. M.
12.00	1.15 A. M.		

EXPLANATION OF SIGNS: *Makes no stop between Baltimore and Washington other cars make stop at Naval Academy Jct.
n Will stop on signal at High Bridge to receive passengers. * Will
stop on signal to Conductor to discharge passengers at Dodge Park.
n Local from Naval Academy Jct.

WASHINGTON AND BALTIMORE
ACCOMMODATION CARS. (Making Local Stops.)

Leave Baltimore.	Arrive Washington.	Leave Washington.	Arrive Baltimore.
6.50 A. M.	8.25 A. M.	6.00 A. M.	7.15 A. M.
9.05	10.30	6.55	8.30
11.00	12.35	9.50	10.45
1.00 P. M.	2.35	11.10	12.45 P. M.
3.00	4.35	1.10 P. M.	2.45
5.00	6.35	3.10	4.45
6.00s	7.15	5.10	6.45
6.15	To N. A. Jct. Only	7.10	8.45
7.00	To N. A. Jct. Only	8.30n	9.45
8.00	9.45 P. M.	6.15	To N. A. Jct. Only
8.50n	To N. A. Jct. Only	9.05 P. M.	11.45 P. M.
9.45	11.45 P. M.	11.40	1.03 A. M.
10.30	To N. A. Jct. Only		
11.00	To N. A. Jct. Only		
12.00	1.15 A. M.		

EXPLANATION OF SIGNS: n Local from Naval Academy Jct.

NAVAL ACADEMY JUNCTION TO WASHINGTON & BALTIMORE.
ACCOMMODATION CARS. (Making Local Stops.)

Leave Naval Academy Jct.	Arrive Baltimore.	Leave Naval Academy Jct.	Arrive Washington.
5.45 A. M.	6.30 A. M.	5.57 A. M.	6.45 A. M.
6.10	6.55	6.45	7.30
7.15	7.50	7.15	8.05

ANNAPOLIS AND ANNAPOLIS JUNCTION.
Connecting with Penna. R. R. at Odenton and A. & W. B. at Annapolis Rd.
READ DOWN Heavy Figures A. M. READ UP

7.18	11.38	3.58	5.30	Lv. Annapolis	Ar.	9.10	1.45	5.15	7.30
7.40	11.37	3.57	5.57	Ar. Naval Acad. Jct.		8.05	1.18	4.45	7.00
7.48	11.50	3.58	5.58		Odenton		8.01	1.17	4.44	6.59
7.57	12.07	4.07	6.07		Portland		8.31	1.08	4.33	6.45
8.02	12.12	4.12	6.12	Ar. Annapolis Jct.	Lv.	7.20	1.03	4.28	6.40

Figure 5. Daily schedule of Washington-Baltimore Rail Service (1909).

the Republican party line that the net result at the conclusion of the process would be meaningful tariff reform, i.e., reduced duties.[11] At the same time, no one in the party, including Mr. Payne, Chairman of the Ways and Means Committee through which it would necessarily pass, so much as hinted at the details of the proposed constitutional amendment that would be advanced within the week. It is not beyond the realm of possibility that one of the decisions made during this trip pertained to the timing of that announcement and the need to expedite it to help reduce the political temperature. A second, less consequential but arguably more certain and more immediate device for improving the tenor of day-to-day life on the Hill, staging the congressional ballgame, something Vreeland and Payne might have already had in mind, could have been on the agenda as well. Anything to reduce the growing animosity in all quarters.

Consider: When CBG1 did take place a short time later, the tariff legislation—and, significantly, the management of the House by Speaker Cannon—were top of mind in much of the news coverage. Some headlines: *The New York Times*: "Baseball Victory for the Democrats: Defeat Republican Members of the House, Getting Revenge for Tariff Treatment;" *Nashville Banner*: "Democrats Score Their Only Victory of the Extra Session: 'Uncle Joe' Cannon Looks on Powerless to Prevent the Minority Walloping the Life Out of the Majority in Congressional Baseball Game;" *The Cincinnati Enquirer*: "Carnage Is Something Awful: Tariff Wrangle is Child's Play Compared to This Sanguinary Struggle."[12]

Consider: The timing of the Baltimore trip and the subsequent playing of CBG1 was almost surely not coincidental. But if John Tener, by every account an ambitious politician, had been the moving force behind the Baltimore trip, it seems likely that he would have placed himself in the same auto as the most powerful of his invitees, Majority Leader Payne. Yet that was not the case. Moreover, since Tener was by no means a central player in the ongoing tariff fight, there is no reason that, left to his own devices, he would have constituted the traveling party as it was, replete with central players in the machinations surrounding the tariff bill. Watson, though still a powerful insider, was not in Congress when Tener arrived and there is no indication the two were acquainted. And only Judge Fisher was a fellow Elk, though there were certainly more members of that association in the House, so a gathering of Elks could not have been the motivation. What Watson and Fisher had in common, however, was that both were actively lobbying to retain protectionist duties. Finally, as for the subsequent congressional game, Tener does not appear to have given much forethought to the composition of the GOP team even a few days before the two sides took the field. Or if he did, and if he had recruited those he named when challenged by Garner, he had been overruled by a higher power, most likely Vreeland. The roster was almost entirely different from the one Tener had listed earlier.

With all of these points in mind, it is less than certain that Tener was in the fullest sense the founding father of CBG1, and at a minimum, entirely reasonable to conclude that he was less the driving force behind the game than a convenient and suitably credentialed and skilled agent for others who saw its potential benefits. Nevertheless, it is surely the case that Tener played an important role in moving the project forward.

BASEBALL IN WASHINGTON:
LOCATION, LOCATION, LOCATION, LOCATION,
LOCATION AND . . . LOCATION

Over hill, over dale,
Thorough bush, thorough brier,
Over park, over pale,
Thorough flood, thorough fire.[1]

DESPITE THE TITLE of his play, *A Midsummer Night's Dream*, chances are
pretty good that William Shakespeare did not have Washington baseball
in mind when he wrote this stanza. English audiences would have to wait
a few centuries for the *Manchester Guardian* to explain even the basics of
the game. But in their way, these lines do tell a tale.

If one thing can be said about major league baseball in Washington,
it is that nothing has come easily. Whether the focus has been on the
owners, the team, the league, the players, or the grounds, every time
things have seemed to be going well, to have settled into a pattern, some
kind of disaster has struck. Teams fail at the box office. Leagues decide
to consolidate, or they collapse. Owners run out of money or patience.
Grandstands burn to the ground. The possibilities have proven endless.
Plus, one can need a scorecard just to keep up with all of the nomen-
clature. The local team might be called the Nationals, the Senators, or
even the Statesmen—*all at the very same time*. And their grounds could
be known as Boundary Field, National Park, National League Park, or
American League Park—appellations that were, at one time or another

and in one combination or another, *all applied to the same ballpark*, or at least to a ballpark at the same physical location. Part of the confusion (today) arises from the relatively loose naming customs of earlier eras, but part arises from the uncertainties of placing a major league franchise in the nation's capital. A rose by any other name? A tale full of sound and fury? Perhaps there really is a Shakespearean element to this sordid history.

Though today's city is bigger, wealthier, and far more sophisticated than it was in the last century, for many years, and certainly in the period before and including 1909 as well as long after, Washington had a dual personality of sorts: It was at once a small city with a limited economic base beyond the federal government (what baseball analysts would today term a small market) and a center of great political power. To appeal to the power, major league baseball, in its various incarnations, repeatedly placed teams in the city. However, because of the city's economic and social limitations, those teams did not survive for long.

The intertwining of the game and the government has been an essential element of professional baseball in Washington from day one, a fact that is reflected in the peripatetic, one might even say star-crossed, ramblings of both the team and the grounds it has called home. A congressional baseball game, a contest between itinerant politicians who happened to have landed in the capital city for a time, at American League Park, by 1909 the ninth home field of the local major leaguers? It was a natural.

Pay-for-play baseball—not quite the professional game—first came to Washington in the form of the Washington Nationals Baseball Club in 1859. By 1867, the team had perfected a sort of hybrid model of amateur baseball that could only be available in the capital city, providing government patronage jobs for all of its players, who thus retained their amateur standing and emerged as something of a powerhouse. Games were split between a field at Sixteenth and S Streets, NW, well north of the White House, and one just south of the executive mansion and attracted extensive and extraordinarily detailed attention in the local media. At the S Street grounds, there were sometimes special problems, to wit: "Ward brought Leavenworth and King home and made his third on a hit to centre field, the ball getting into a flock of sheep, which scattered precipitately and got in the way of the players, notwithstanding the careful attention of a stalwart policeman, who acted as shepherd."[2]

The Nationals undertook a precedent-setting tour from July 10, 1867, through the end of that month, visiting a number of cities in what was then regarded as "the west."[3] Typical of the journey was their reception in Louisville, Kentucky, where the local newspaper advertised a "grand match" by observing,

> It will be remembered that the "Nationals" started last week upon their tour to dispute any pretensions with, and establish their claim against, rival clubs upon the field of green as champions of the west and south. They will doubtless do this successfully, as the club is considered to be one of the best in the country, and their record so far shows them to be almost invincible.[4]

Upon their return to the capital in July, one news account reported that appreciation for their efforts and demeanor had been accorded throughout their travels and called for a welcome-home celebration."[5]

Alas, that may have been the high point of baseball in Washington for more than half a century. From that point forward, the team could not find a stable league association, could not find a consistent home field, and could not win baseball games with any regularity. And its erstwhile partner, the federal government, was not always helpful.

The first *recorded* Nationals game was played May 5, 1869, on a field then called the White (House) Lot, the area south of the White House now known as the Ellipse. The Ellipse is the site today of the Zero Milestone, the point from which all U.S. highway road distances from the capital are measured.

In 1884, the Nationals joined the American Association, regarded at the time as a "major" league, but the team folded mid-season. Later that summer, the team joined the short-lived Union Association.

When the Union Association disbanded before the start of the 1885 season, the Nationals were left homeless, but in 1886, the team was accepted for the first time into the National League, which dated its claim to "major league" status to 1876, where they remained through 1889 before being eliminated in a reorganization.

Figure 6. Baseball was still played on the Ellipse (The White Lot) in 1945.

In 1890, even the rebel Players League did not have a place for a team in Washington. It did, however, have a place for Washington's former players; they became the core of the Buffalo entry in the rebel league.[6]

After a December 1890 organizational meeting at Willard's Hall in 1891, the newly renamed Washington Statesmen, also still called the Nationals, joined the American Association, prompting one local newspaper to opine, "The base-ball agony is over."[7] And in their very first game in the new league they drew a crowd of some 2,500 fans, many of whom had journeyed down from Baltimore to support the opposing Orioles. The home team scored a 7-5 victory.[8] It appeared to be an auspicious start, but alas, that entire league folded following the season.

From 1892 through 1899, a newly branded Washington Senators club found a new place in the then-twelve-team National League. But when the National League consolidated from twelve to eight teams in 1900, Washington *again* lost at the game of musical chairs.

Still, by 1909, Washington's baseball fans had reason for optimism, if not for the performance of their team on the field, at least for the durability of their home field. It was only in 1901, when the newly renamed American League claimed major league status and included the Senators among its eight charter members, that the prospects for stability seemed genuinely promising. And, though the capital city's travails would continue in the years ahead, that is where matters stood in 1909.[9]

Through all of this, the Washington teams developed a distinguished fan base that included several U.S. presidents. President Andrew Johnson, for example, was frequently seen at the games at the White Lot and even occupied a private section of the grandstand that team owner and Senator Arthur Pue Gorman had set aside for him. During one contest against the Excelsior Club of New York, Johnson even held a reception for the team in the grandstand with entertainment provided by the Marine Corps band. President Ulysses Grant was also a regular at the White Lot until a series of brawls between whites and blacks caused him to close the grounds. During the team's National League years, President Benjamin Harrison and his Treasury Secretary, Charles Foster, were also frequent visitors to Washington's games, choosing to sit in the press section and eating peanuts as they conversed.[10] Professional baseball teams typically develop close relationships with their respective local business communities, and that was very much the case here. The only difference? The local business in Washington is the federal government and those who would deal with it.

Presidential patronage notwithstanding, the home grounds for highest-level baseball in the capital changed almost as frequently as the team names and league affiliations.[11] The aforementioned White House Lot was home to the early Nationals team beginning in 1867, but the team shared the grounds with two others and had access for games only twice a week, on Mondays and Thursdays.[12] That was the reason they also played at the unnamed field at Sixteenth and S Streets, where it was not only their fans who flocked to the site.

In 1884, when the Nationals played first in the American Association, the games were held at a field known as Athletic Park, distant from the city center and close to the eastern-most corner boundary of the diamond-shaped District of Columbia; that spot is home today to the Maya Angelou Public Charter School.

Upon joining the Union Association later that same year, the team made its home at the Capitol Grounds, also known as Union Association

Grounds, located just northeast of the Capitol Building, which had a capacity of 6,000. Today, that location is occupied by the Russell Senate Office Building.

During its stint in the National League from 1886-1889, Washington again played its games near the center of town and just north of the Capitol, but this time in a location known technically as Swampoodle Grounds and more broadly as Capital Park Grounds, located where today we find Columbus Circle and Union Station. The capacity of that park was again around 6,000 spectators; the signature element of the facility was its outfield walls, which rose some twenty feet into the air. When the team once again lost its affiliation in 1890, albeit briefly, the owners of that property put it on the market. Once again, enter the government.

Up until it was granted home rule status in 1973, local government in the District of Columbia was actively overseen by Congress and its committees, with day-to-day control vested in a group of three Commissioners, one from each major party and one from the Army Corps of Engineers, appointed by the President. This meant that federal interests were often interlocked with local interests in both policy and politics. This governing structure came into play in 1890 when the city was left without a major league baseball team for what turned out to be a single year. The abandonment of the baseball grounds just north of the Capitol created an open space close to the center of government, something Congress could not ignore. So, the first week in January 1891, the Senate Committee on Printing commenced hearings to determine the suitability of the site for a new Government Printing Office (GPO) edifice. Within weeks, the Senators had reported not only that the location was suitable for such a project but that the ground itself could support a building of any size and weight.[13] As matters later developed, the new GPO facility was built elsewhere. But in 1891, with Congress weighing the potentialities, the owners of Swampoodle Grounds were expecting a lucrative sale to the government. So, the "new" (again) Washington Nationals/Senators of 1891, on the cusp of joining the American Association, would need to look elsewhere for their home grounds. That is when the location that would eventually house American League Park and host the first congressional baseball game came to the fore.

Here is the timeline of events beginning the week after the Senate committee announced its intentions to acquire the old ballpark location.

- January 12. Representatives of the American Association (association president Allen W. Thurman, Baltimore Orioles owner William "Bald Billy" Barnie, and St. Louis and Cincinnati owner Chris von der Ahe) and the National League (Chicago White Stockings owner Al Spalding, Brooklyn Bridegrooms owner Charles Byrne, and New York Giants owner John B. Day) met in New York to pick over the bones of the defunct Players League and framed a new governing agreement including a recommitment to the reserve rule.[14]

- January 16. Michael Scanlon, who had represented Washington at the New York meetings, proclaimed that "We are in the American Association, and way up in it, too." He then noted that "we have an option on the old park, corner 7th Street and Boundary, and it is of all the locations available, the one we wanted. It can be reached by the cable cars and the 9th Street cars." He went on to describe the plans for a one-story horseshoe-shaped grandstand and some of the associated costs.[15]

- January 17. Mr. Scanlon released a few more details of the field and the arrangements in a separate interview.

  The National Club will next season occupy the old Schuet-zen Park. . . . A few more preliminaries have yet to be arranged before the ten years' lease is consummated. . . . The dimensions are all that could be desired, there being a mean depth of 800 feet, with a clear width of 400 feet, making the largest park devoted to base ball in America. The cable cars will take passengers to the grounds from Pennsylvania Avenue in sixteen minutes, the Metropolitan from Ninth and F Street in twenty-two minutes. As soon as the lease is completed workmen will commence putting them in condition.[16]

- January 24. There was no further progress to report on the ballpark, Mr. Scanlon told the press, but it was reassuring that the new Washington team was backed by a syndicate of thirty businessmen who had "placed their hard cash in the treasury" and planned to run the team on a businesslike basis.[17]

• January 29. The National Baseball Club announced that it had signed a five-year lease for what was then described as Baier's (or Beyer's) Seventh Street Park, with work to begin the following week to clear the trees and erect the grandstand.[18]

At this point, we would do well to clarify the name of the park in question. The District of Columbia was created in the shape of a diamond, and except for the area west of the Potomac River that was later ceded back to Virginia, it has retained that shape. However, in 1891, the

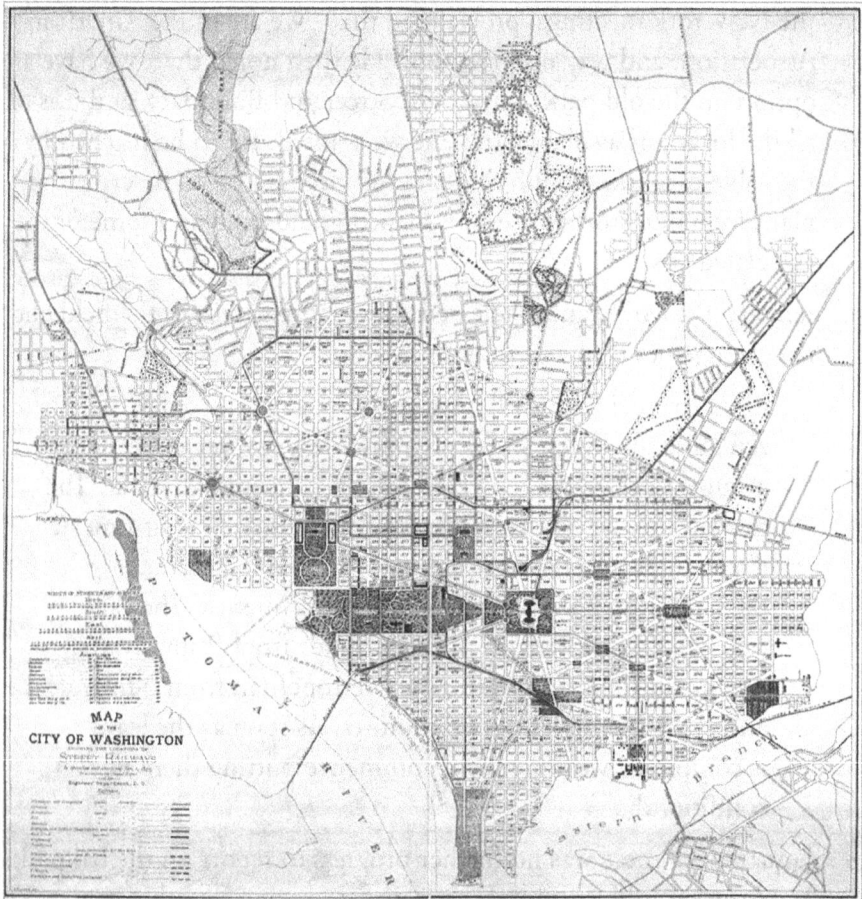

Figure 7. Washington, DC, map showing street rail lines (1895).

city of Washington was not coterminous with the District; it was smaller. And what amounted to the northern city limit from Rock Creek Park around to more or less the midpoint of the city was delimited by the arc of Boundary Road, soon to be renamed Florida Avenue. The area selected for the new ballpark in 1891 lay within the District but just across Boundary Road, and thus outside the city, at about the point where Seventh Street, NW, intersected it. It's formal historical name notwithstanding, whether Schuetzen's or Baier's Park, it was known commonly as Boundary Field. The map in Figure 7, dated a few years later, shows the existing street railways in 1891. To locate the ballpark site, go to the absolute center of the map, then look northward about one-third of the way along the fold to the point where a rail line can be seen turning to the northwest and then to the west. The open lot to the immediate east of that initial turn was the location of Boundary Field.

- February 1. The *Washington Herald* celebrated progress on the ballpark:

  The affairs of the National Base-Ball Club reached a much better shape yesterday, when the trustee of the old Schuetzen Park, Mr. Enoch Totten, and the agent of the ball club, Mr. T.B. Kalbfus, closed their negotiations for a lease, and placed the paper on record in City Hall. Many erroneous statements have been made lately in regard to the affairs of the club, especially the location of the park. . . . The grandstand will not be up against the Freedmen's Hospital [see below]; it will be many yards away. The grounds are to be the prettiest in America and will rival the famous old White Lot.[19]

- February 5. Bids for work on the new ballpark were set to be opened the following day, with work beginning immediately. The grandstand would be a three-sided structure designed to accommodate twelve to fifteen hundred people, with a hundred-foot-long center section and two fifty-foot extensions at angles of about thirty degrees. Two bleachers would be built, one on either side but the largest to the south, to seat an additional five thousand. Contrary to the original plan [note this reference], the grandstand would be built back to the west with batting from the west to the east. The proximity to mass transit notwithstanding, it was apparent that not everyone would journey to the park by that means. "Owing to the amplitude of the park, which contains much more room than is really needed, the stands will not be next to the fences on any side, and there will be plenty of space all around for the hitching of horses. . . ."[20] All was expected to be ready by April 1.

- February 6. Welcome to Washington I. An objection was raised as to the ballpark's constituting a public nuisance. The objection came from Dr. C. M. Purvis, the resident physician (chief officer) at Freedmen's Hospital, which, if the ballpark were built, would find itself adjacent to the right [actually, the left] field fence [after the originally planned direction of play had been reversed]. To appreciate the objection, we need to realize something else about Washington, DC, in 1909 that we have not yet touched upon. The city was, as it had always been, a segregated city with a Jim Crow culture typical of the era.

> In 1863, following Lincoln's Emancipation Proclamation, Freedmen's Hospital had been established in Washington to provide patient care and professional training for African Americans, including newly freed slaves. Ever since Howard University had been founded four years later, in 1867, the two institutions had been tightly bound to one another. In those days, the city was crowded, tense, and not well prepared for modernization, either physically or culturally. Initially the hospital was administered by the military and located on the grounds of Camp Barker at Thirteenth and R Streets, NW. The administration then passed to the Freedmen's Bureau, and in 1869, construction was begun at a new location at Fifth and W Streets, adjacent to the university, on land that had previously been a German beer hall associated in some way with Schuetzen Park, but at the end farthest away from Boundary Road. In 1908, the hospital would begin replacing its wooden buildings with a more modern plant that survives to this day. Freedmen's Hospital was the origin point for today's Howard University Hospital.[21] Now, back to our main story.

It was within this context that Purvis wrote a letter to the Secretary of the Interior objecting to the use of the land for such a "nefarious" purpose that would bring the patrons of base ball, "the worst element of society," to an area near the hospital where peace and quiet should prevail. Secretary Noble passed Purvis's letter to the District Commissioners along with his concurrence. This led to a public uproar as both sides prepared for battle.[22] The club hired an attorney by the name of Sutherland to argue its case, which had two basic elements: (a) that objecting to a possible nuisance on hypothetical grounds before it was proven to be an actual nuisance was legally inappropriate and (b) that, even if the ballpark were a nuisance to the patients of the hospital, every city tolerates multiple activities and hence multiple low-level nuisances. Besides, the argument went, the grandstand that would be generating the noise was at the far end of the property from the hospital campus.[23]

- February 9. The National Base Ball Club of Washington, H.B. Bennett, president, obtained an operating charter from the District's corporation court.[24]

- February 12. At least one entrepreneur, recognizing an opportunity, offered for rent a store on Seventh Street, NW, near the cable rail terminus, noting, "The location of the new base ball park just north of this property increases its business advantages.[25]

- February 13. Welcome to Washington II, Friday the Thirteenth Edition. Dr. Purvis addressed the Commission, stating his concern, followed by Mr. Kalbfus representing the ball club, who argued that the real nuisance to the hospital was presented by the picnic parties that were then common in the park near the hospital during summer evenings and that the construction and operation of the ballpark would immediately abate this nuisance, thus serving the interests of the hospital patients. Kalbfus then proposed to abandon construction of the north bleachers, compensating by extending the south bleachers, and Purvis accepted the amended plan.[26] Having weighed the issue, the District Commissioners concluded that Dr. Purvis had no good argument against the ballpark and directed their Inspector Entwistle to give the permit to the contractor who had been selected for the work, a Mr. Dunn. Work was to begin the following Monday.[27]

- February 16. Welcome to Washington III. The District Commission granted the Washington Base Ball Club an unrestricted permit to *build* the stands and seats at the new ballpark. The Commission cautioned, however, that it retained the right to deny the team a license to *operate* if it turned out that the park did, in fact, constitute a nuisance detrimental to the welfare of the patients in the hospital.[28] The game and the associated posturing, having been played out in full, work commenced immediately.

- February 18. The American Association fired Allen Thurman as its president and withdrew from its agreement with the National League, renewing the warfare between the two and restarting the competition for players. Mr. Thurman denounced the Association's "treachery" and vowed that the group would never again be associated with the National League and its newest partner, the Western Association.[29]

- February 28. While the American Association was trying to sort out its affairs, construction continued at the new ballpark, though rain had slowed progress. Mr. Dunn indicated he would add more workers to get back on schedule. Already, the fences were under way and the tree cutters had cleared enough land to allow construction to begin on the grandstand. The main task ahead was to be the grading of the field, which formerly had been occupied by a mature stand of 125 large oak trees.[30] More trees remained uncut just beyond the twenty-foot-high walls, and hanging branches would sometimes interfere with fly balls (e.g., by knocking down prospective home runs and keeping the balls in play), but that was a problem for the future.[31]

- March 3. The National League met to formulate its schedule for the coming season, and to decide how aggressively to fight the American Association's signing of players still under contract to National League teams. Mr. Thurman, who, despite his firing by the Association, was still nominally the chairman of the National Board of Control that had been established under its defunct agreement with the National League, told Association President Chris Van der

Ahe, his replacement, that he would be "on the stool of repentance inside of a month." The Association was set to meet to plan its own schedule.[32]

- March 7. The Washington team decided to change its local advertising from using posters to placing painted wooden billboards around the city updated to give notice of each day's game. The signs could also be used to advise patrons if conditions at the grounds made play unlikely. Admission was set at twenty-five cents. Alas, two snowstorms had seriously slowed construction at the ballpark, putting the timely completion of the stands and fences and the grading of the field in jeopardy.[33]

- March 23. It became clear that construction of the ballpark was far behind schedule, and the projected April 1 opening was beyond reach. The earlier snows had been followed by frequent rain, leaving the ground so wet as to be unworkable. The trees had been cleared, and the stands and fences were nearly completed, but finishing work had stalled.[34]

- April 10. Progress. The contractor was paid in full and handed over the keys to the ballpark. All was in readiness, and the first official home game was to be played on Monday, April 13, weather permitting. Surveyors, fans were assured, had "laid off a diamond that is true to the thousandth of an inch."[35]

- April 13. The new ballpark, known as Boundary Field, which, after considerably more anguish, would house the first congressional baseball game in 1909, officially opened. Four thousand people watched the game in vibrant sunshine. The Washington Statesmen, as they were known that year, were shut out by the Boston Americans (the future Red Sox), losing by the score of 6-0. The team would finish the season with a record of 44-91. The modern era of Washington Baseball had begun.[36]

At the conclusion of the 1891 season, the American Association collapsed and died.

Still, all was not lost. In 1892, the Washington Statesmen, renamed the Senators and also known as the Washington Nationals, rejoined the

National League, where they remained until 1899. As the earlier con-
tretemps with the neighboring hospital suggested, during these years,
Washington remained culturally a segregated city. In 1895, for example,
the club placed the following advertisement:

> WANTED—10 Boys and 4 colored men to sell refreshments on
> base ball grounds; boys must bring 50 cents to pay on account of
> uniform required: Apply after 2 p.m. NATIONAL BASE BALL
> PARK.[37]

Through that time, Boundary Field, sometimes called National Park,
remained the team's home. But in 1900, when the National League consolidated from twelve teams to eight, Washington *again* found itself on
the outside looking in.

Toward the end of its National League run, the team was not doing
well financially, and the league was concerned about its revenues. In
November 1899, the Wagner brothers, residents of Philadelphia who
owned a controlling interest in the Washington club at that point
(as well as in two other National League teams), were approached by
Michael Scanlon, who had owned the team during its earlier stint in
the National League and who sought to build a consortium of local fans
to purchase the team. Scanlon mailed postcards to local fans, inviting
them to an organizational meeting at the Willard Hotel on the evening of
the sixteenth. The Wagners signaled their openness to sell the team, the
National League franchise, the lease on the ballpark, which would expire
in 1901, and all of the players' contracts for a total of $30,000.

The president of the National League offered his encouragement, but
the deal was apparently clouded by the prospect of moving to a different
playing field. The league had a requirement that its ballparks must be
reachable from the city center within a certain time limit. But a local
railway line had already signed a contract committing to build a new
ballpark at a different and more distant site, enclose the grounds, erect
a suitable grandstand, and create a first-class baseball diamond, all of
this to be provided free of charge to the team under its new ownership
so long as it would agree to play its games on the new grounds with
the other National League clubs as opponents.[38] The incentive for the

railway company was to create an attraction to which it largely controlled access. Accepting this very attractive arrangement, however, put the Scanlon group at odds with the site-selection rules of the league, which, in turn, could withhold the very recognition on which the deal was conditioned—the right to play against National League competition.

The deal with the Scanlon syndicate fell through rather quickly, and the Wagners announced that the club was no longer for sale at any price. This proved to be a bad move. In December, the National League held discussions about scaling back from twelve teams to eight by eliminating the Washington team along with those in Baltimore, Cleveland, and Louisville. Earl Wagner was on hand to lobby against such a move, but the situation was very much up in the air.[39] Not for long. In late January 1900, after suggesting to the other owners that Washington might not go quietly into that goodnight, Earl Wagner stated publicly that the Senators would continue as members of the National League, which would be reduced to ten teams by the elimination of Cleveland and Louisville.[40] But then, in February 1900, Wagner announced that the league had approached him to name his price for a terminal buyout of the franchise and that, after he demanded a payment that was clearly taken as unreasonable, Washington was simply forced out of the National League without compensation, though he was allowed to sell his players' contracts to other teams for whatever they might bring. Beyond that, the Wagners were left with little more than the lease on Boundary Field.[41]

In the meantime, under the leadership of Ban Johnson and Charley Comiskey, the former Western League had renamed itself the American League and, planning to benefit from the paring of teams from the National League, prepared to proclaim itself a "major" circuit, which it did in 1901. In a November 1900 meeting in Chicago, John J. McGraw agreed to organize an American League team in Baltimore, which had, together with Washington, lost out in the final thinning of the National League. James Manning, owner of the Kansas City Blues team that he planned to move to the nation's capital, represented Washington in the same meeting. At the time, a rival Washington ownership syndicate had lined up local capital and a ballpark and was planning to join yet another outlaw league called the National Association. That Association was scheming to prevent Manning from creating an American League contender in the city that would compete for fan support.[42] In January 1901, the American League held meetings in New York to work toward a final structure, after which Ban Johnson toured several of the League's accepted and prospective cities. He and Manning jointly visited Washington, where the need to lock in suitable baseball grounds became paramount.[43]

Confused yet? Just think about the fans in Washington around that time.

Manning was able to close a deal for that new park, to be known as American League Park, in short order. The Wagners still held the lease to Boundary Field and had no interest in making it available, least of all to a team in the upstart American League. Manning hoped instead to locate the ballpark on an old circus lot on North Capitol Street, but he was unable to resolve the problem presented by another street that bisected the property. In addition, agents of the National League were generating petition drives against the North Capitol Street site in an effort to slow the development of the rival circuit by denying it a close-in location. Manning settled instead on a piece of land distant from the middle of town at Fourteenth and H Streets, NE, for which he had been negotiating in secret for some time.

This caused some initial concern because the new park would be accessible by only one street railway, the Columbia line, but supporters pointed out that five other lines provided easy transfer to Columbia trains, and that seemed to calm the critics. The lot selected was to be leased from the Washington Brick Machine Company and was pitted and covered with rubbish that needed to be cleared before the field could be filled in and the stands erected.[44] By February 21, workers were hard at work grading the new site, which involved taking two and a half feet off the surface of the eastern side of the lot and using the dirt to fill a big hole where left field would be. This site preparation was undertaken by the brick company rather than by Manning, and the company promised to have the grading completed by April 1. Manning indicated he would be seeking construction bids before month's end so that building work could be underway by the first week of March.[45]

From that point forward, matters went relatively smoothly, at least in Washington baseball terms. The Senators joined the American League, where they would reside for the next several decades, but needless to say, the new ballpark was not ready in time for opening day. Instead, the team would have been forced to play its inaugural pair of American League home games at Georgetown University.[46] But this proved unnecessary: both were rained out. It wasn't until April 29, over a week later, that the team was able to play on its new grounds; literally just hours after the final nail was driven into the left field bleachers and the last load of dirt was dumped on the infield. Early in the afternoon, the Washington players, clad in new white uniforms, were driven in carriages to Riggs House, a hotel at Fifteenth and G Streets in downtown Washington, where the visiting team from Baltimore was staying. At two o'clock, a parade stepped off in the direction of the ballpark, headed by Haley's Band in a large omnibus. At the ballpark, they found a large crowd, as well as league president Ban Johnson, awaiting their arrival. Everything was finally coming up roses.[47]

Unfortunately, over the next three seasons, large crowds proved to be the exception. As had been speculated early on, the distance of the park from the center city and the need to transfer rail lines was apparently a factor. In addition, there were issues with the playing surface at American League Park, especially in the outfield. But the killer seemed to be another government intervention—a law passed by Congress requiring all federal workers, the team's principal patrons, to remain on the job until at least 4:30 in the afternoon, a requirement that made it impossible for many to reach the distant ballpark by game time. At that point, an effort to sell the team to yet another new ownership group fell through, and the league, in the person of Ban Johnson, took operational control in 1904.

In light of these developments and given the fact that the previous lease held by the Wagners had finally expired and not been renewed, attention had turned again to the possibility of moving the team back to the Boundary Field site. That, it was believed, would add as many as five hundred fans to the attendance at each game. There had been preliminary steps toward that end during the pending sale of the club, but those had resulted in hard feelings on the part of the Totten estate that controlled the lease. Still, Johnson believed that particular problem could be overcome, and that the old park, which was in decline from inattention, could be renovated easily. New fences and bleachers could be built, he thought, and little work would be needed on the playing surface.[48]

By March 24, the team had been sold to a new local ownership group headed by William J. Dwyer and Thomas C. Noyes, and a lease had been acquired for the old National League facility at Boundary Field. On a tour of the grounds, a news reporter observed that the field proper was in good condition but that there was more work to do than had been expected. The wooden fences in center and right fields, for example, had been carried off by the neighbors for kindling. A contractor named Harvey was set to begin work on the fences and bleachers, but the permit for that work was being held up due to protests filed with the District Commission by several adjacent property owners. Today we would call them NIMBYs—Not In My Back Yard. The neighbors demanded that the Commissioners annul the permit they had granted to construct the grandstand and other seats and prevent the granting of a license for the games. They based their demands on the assertion that the structures would violate the District's fire regulations, that the shouting and other noise of the games would constitute a public nuisance, that allowing the construction would eliminate the potential to extend Elm and Sixth Streets through the grounds (which had never been contemplated), and that the project should be treated under the regulations that required permission from nearby property owners before the introduction of a merry-go-round or circus. Oh, yes. Lest we forget, the challengers also noted at the last minute that the noise from the games would disturb the patients at Freedmen's Hospital. The club replied that no nuisance could

Figure 8. A game at American League Park, Washington, DC (1905).

be assumed without evidence and that if one occurred, the neighbors could litigate at that time. In other words, the arguments in 1904 had a certain similarity to those made nearly fifteen years earlier.[49] These issues were resolved, as one might expect, by a project-affirming vote of the Commission. But then, of course, another problem arose.

Unfortunately, under their earlier owners, the Senators had signed a five-year lease on the brickyard property that became American League Park. And when news of the new arrangement became public, Washington Brick filed suit in Equity Court Number 2, claiming that the team still owed it $2500 for last year's rental and that its only collateral was the grandstand at the ballpark.[50] By March 29, the club owners were expressing optimism that they would be able to reach an agreement with the brick company, and by the next day, that had come to pass, and the court had lifted the injunction that prevented work on the old site.[51] On the thirty-first, workers began tearing down the seats and roof of the stands at American League Park and moving the entire structure, in pieces, to Boundary Field. Remarkably, the demolition and transfer were accomplished in about one day. In the meantime, Jim O'Day, the groundskeeper at the old/new park, was getting the playing surface in order.[52] The result was a new version of Boundary Field that was to serve as the home of the Washington Senators of the American League, and that would, in 1909, host the very first congressional baseball game.

CBG 1: SCHEDULING THE GAME

BY 1909, AND following the custom of the time, Boundary Field had become known colloquially as American League Park, not to be confused with the brickyard ballpark that had borne the same name. The sectional map in Figure 9 shows the outline of the ballpark (center) just to the northeast of the major intersection of Florida Avenue (previously Boundary Road), running southeast to northwest, and Georgia Avenue running to the north. Note the presence in 1909 of the north-side bleachers, the construction of which had earlier been nixed. The building to the immediate north of the end of those bleachers was the first permanent building of the Freedmen's Hospital, used as well by Howard University. The complex of buildings immediately west of the hospital constituted a lumber yard that would later play a cameo role in our tale.

Any reader who has ever stepped onto a Major League baseball field, even for just a moment, or taken one of those tours that include visits to a dugout and a clubhouse—perhaps even the batting cages or the bullpen—will understand the allure of such a place. That was no less true in 1909 than it is today, and given that we are speaking here about members of Congress—even with exceptions arguably the largest single collection of egos and senses of entitlement on the planet—there was only one place in Washington that would be seen as suitable to host a congressional baseball game: American League Park. But those congressmen were not the only ones to feel the magnetism of the ballpark. When not in use by the Senators squad, the field was in great demand.

A League of Their Own. In 1909, African Americans were many years away from participating in Major League baseball, and even the formation

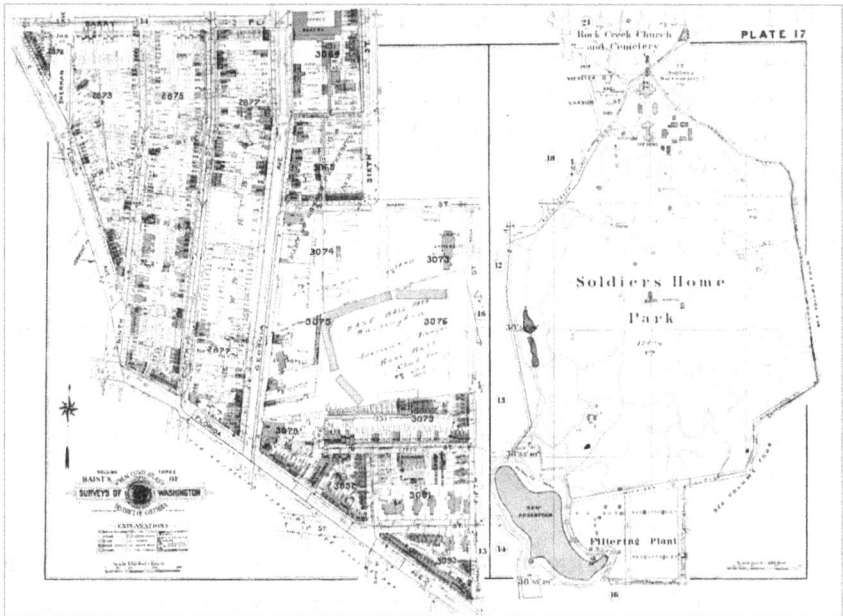

Figure 9. Map showing location of American League Park (1909).

of the Negro National League was still a decade in the future. But Washington had an active mixed amateur and professional African American baseball community with teams that contended for championships both locally and with others up and down the east coast. Teams like the Piedmont White Sox and the Belmonts competed for players and local approbation.[1] The big story of African American baseball in the District in 1909 was the formation of the Washington Giants baseball team.

The Washington Giants were incorporated in April 1909 with capital stock valued at $5000. The team, which planned to play at home only when the American League team was on the road, had arranged to compete in the Independent Professional Baseball Teams of America and Cuba circuit against such teams as the Cuban Stars, Brooklyn Royal Giants, Philadelphia Giants, Cuban Giants, Leland Giants of Chicago, and others, and held an option to play at Union League Park, not to be confused with Union Association Grounds where the Nationals had played briefly in 1894.[2] As noted, that site had been claimed by Congress, not for a new printing office building as originally intended, but for the first Senate office building, later named for Richard Russell, which was built between 1903 and 1908 and opened for occupancy in

1909. Rather, this was likely the field used by the ill-fated Washington team in the Union League of Professional Baseball Clubs, an outlaw circuit (operating outside of the National Agreement that governed major league and affiliated teams) founded by Alfred Lawson in Philadelphia in December 1907.[3]

The Washington entry in that league, led by president William F. Hart, managed by Arthur Irwin, and captained by Charley Atherton, began play in April 1908 at a new ballpark constructed at Fifteenth Street and Florida Avenue, NE—essentially the same east-end location as the original American League Park.[4] Per the custom, the grounds were known as Union League Park.

Lawson set out his intentions for the new circuit in a March 28, 1908, interview.

> "Here in Washington, we believe that we have all East Washington solidly with us, and we believe that we will furnish such a quality of ball that residents of other sections of the city will also come down."[5]

East-end support or not, this was still Washington. The Union League disbanded on June 3, 1908, after just two months of play.[6] But bad news for some may be good news for others. There was a vacant professional-level baseball field available in 1909. The Washington Giants took an option on that field and began selling additional shares in the team, placing a display advertisement in the *Washington Evening Star* that read: "A Few More SHARES of the WASHINGTON GIANTS, Colored Professional Base Ball Club (Incorporated) is now on sale . . . Shares, 25c each."[7]

On the field, the team found immediate success. In August, they defeated the Piedmont White Sox in a doubleheader to win the District "colored" championship.[8] They were in line for a three-way playoff for the title of "colored champions of the world," but under the arrangements in place, the victory of the Brooklyn Royal Giants over the Philadelphia Giants eliminated the opportunity for a follow-up challenge from Washington. In its stead, the Washington Giants closed out their season with a contest against the Belmonts.[9] In the meantime, the team advertised that it was holding a few dates open for games against "strong white teams," though it is not clear whether there were any takers.[10]

This is of interest in the present context because, in addition to playing most of their games at Union League Field, the Washington Giants also played on occasion at American League Park. For example, while the Nationals were away in Boston for a July 4 series against the Red Sox, the Giants paired off against the Piedmont White Sox in a game at the park on July 5. An added attraction was that the returns from the Washington-Boston contest, taking place at the same hour, would be read out inning-by-inning from the scoreboard aided by a special telegraph wire from Boston.[11]

Amateurs, Young and Old. This was but one of the overlapping uses of American League Park in 1909. For example, a number of high school baseball games were scheduled there beginning in late April.[12] In addition, Washington had an extensive structure of amateur baseball leagues, including the Marquette League, the Departmental League (comprising five teams of African American workers from the Government Printing Office, Bureau of Engraving, War & Navy, Interior Department, and Municipal employees), the Capital City League, the Independence League, the Suburban League, the Sunday School League, the Railroad League, and the Bankers League—enough so that these were divided into two classes based on the quality of play much in the way that high school teams are classified today. Each class had its own city championship competition, and in 1909, all of these championship games were scheduled for American League Park.[13]

Knowing the Drill, Shooting to Thrill. In May 1909, the ballpark hosted the fifteenth annual competition of the Separate Battalion of High School Cadets, a drill team and shooting competition pitting cadets from the city's five black high schools against one another. This was a major event in the African American community that drew an estimated seven thousand "wildly enthusiastic" spectators to the park. The stands were organized into school-specific contingents of friends and relatives of the cadets waving flags with the respective schools' colors. It began with the parading of each company through the city streets to American League Park, led by the Metropolitan Band. The competition required fifty-three separate maneuvers, among them volley firing and skirmish advancement with rapid-fire accompaniment. Each round of shots produced cheers from the crowd. The competition was judged by cavalry Lieutenant Benjamin O. Davis, military instructor at Wilberforce

University, who was the first African American private in the regular army to obtain a commission while in the ranks, and Lieutenants James Walker and Thomas Jones of the District of Columbia National Guard. Awards to the winning company were presented by William V. Cox, vice president of the board of education, other representatives of the school board, and two members of the House representing the committees that governed the District. At the conclusion of the drill, the companies joined in a dress parade led by the Howard University band. The event garnered considerable attention in the city's major newspapers but scarcely a passing mention in the local African American newspaper, the *Washington Bee*, which had similarly ignored the Washington Giants and the other black baseball teams.[14] The previous week American League Park had hosted the parallel competition among drill teams from the city's white technical, business, and high schools, which was greeted by equal spectacle, fanfare, and enthusiasm. In this instance, the judges were three officers of the Army Corps of Engineers clad in dress whites.[15]

The Grounds as Gridiron. Even college football got into the act. The Hatchetites of The George Washington University were set to play the first two home games of their season at Union League Field, and then, once the Nationals season had ended, would play the remainder of their games at American League Park, where they had also played in 1908. In the event, the Nationals season ended early, as usual, and the footballers were able to play all eight of their games at the ballpark, finishing their season with a 3-4-1 record. "All the members of the team," it was reported, appreciated "the conveniences which they enjoyed there—the hot showers and locker rooms in the clubhouse and the softness of the ground, which made it easier for the backs when they were heavily thrown."[16]

The point of this extended recital is simply this. Arranging on short notice to play the first congressional baseball game at American League Park in the very middle of the baseball season amidst a plethora of competing claims was not as simple a matter as it may at first seem. It entailed much more than simply choosing rosters. To begin with, a date needed to be determined that was compatible not only with the home team's schedule but with all of the other scheduled uses of their home field. Once a suitable open date had been identified, the grounds needed to be reserved. That involved not only contacting the club's management but also contracting for use of the facility. It involved staffing of the park—cleanup of the grandstand, bleachers, and restrooms before and after the game, groundskeepers to smooth and mark the field, providing for refreshments, souvenir or merchandise vendors (if any), ticket-takers, and the like—and either recruiting volunteers or compensating the workers, not to mention the planning and oversight of all of these tasks. It required the printing in advance of tickets and (as we shall see) free passes, and the selling of the former and appropriate distribution of the latter. It involved the selection of the charities that would benefit from the gate and paying out of the proceeds. It may have involved coordinating with the local street railway companies that serviced the park. It involved contacting local and national newspapers, some of which did cover the game at some length. Put most simply, this was no walk in the park.

Considering all of this, the focus on John Tener as the primary organizer of CBG1 comes even more into question. Tener was a freshman congressman who, we know, was not familiar with Washington except as an occasional visitor. He certainly had a personal network of old baseball friends, but the Nationals team of 1909 was managed off the field by men of a different era in the game. And even if he had been able to use his contacts to arrange the playing date, he lacked the staff to have addressed in such a brief time the many sordid details of scheduling the event. Certainly, he was not inclined to do that level of work himself. For Tener, the challenge would have been overwhelming.

But for someone else like, say, the Speaker of the House or a long-tenured committee chairman like Sereno Payne, with the contacts, the staff, and, importantly, the influence to make this happen, it would have been a simple matter. After all, in 1909, Congress still exercised more or less direct control over the governing of the District of Columbia. And as for the team's cooperation, surely a call from such an important person would ensure maximum cooperation. So, as before, we might do well to view Mr. Tener's role in initiating the game with a measure of reserve.

DATE	DAY	ACTION
JUL 16	124	The First Congressional Baseball Game is played at American League Park

Tick. Tock.

SENATORS' JOINT IRRESOLUTION
(S. J. I. 18)

WHILE THE SCHEDULING of CBG1 had much to do with the congressional calendar, and specifically the pressures being generated by the slow movement of (and probably by the rumors associated with) the tariff bill and the very recent passage by the House of Senate Joint Resolution 40, the income tax amendment, it was constrained primarily, though among other factors, by the home-and-away schedule of the Nationals baseball team. So, just where were the Nationals on the afternoon of July 16, 1909?

In trouble, that's where.

From the time the Washington team joined the American League in 1901 through the 1908 campaign, success on the field had been a distant dream, if not a pure fantasy. The Senators or Nationals, by either moniker, were losers in the purest sense of the word. The team compiled an overall record of 438 wins and 723 losses, lost more than 100 games twice, never had a winning season, and finished last three times and never higher than sixth in the standings of the eight-team league. It was at the midpoint of this truly miserable performance that baseball commentator and general wag Charley Dryden quipped, "Washington. First in war, first in peace, and last in the American League." He also observed that "Defeat to them is the same as death and taxes to other people."[1] And in July 1909, Washington was playing to its by-then customary standard on the way to a record of 42-110 and yet another last-place finish.

On the sixteenth of July, the team was in Detroit for the fourth game of a series against the Tigers, who were on the way to a pennant-winning

Figure 10. Opening Day, 1909. Left to Right: Joe Cantillon (Mgr.), Bill Shipke (IF), Jesse Tannehill (OF/P), Burt Keeley (P), Bob Gainley (OF), Wid Conroy (3B), Clyde Milan (CF), Red Killefer (OF), Cliff Blankenship (C), Jimmy Delahanty (2B), Bob Un-glaub (UT), Gabby Street (C), George McBride (SS), Doc Gessler (OF), "Sleepy" Bill Burns (P), Jerry Freeman (IF), Bob Groom (P), Tom Hughes (P), Charlie Smith (P), Jerry Edinger (Trainer), Walter Johnson (P). Johnson was suffering from a bad cold, which explains the hat and overcoat. He did not pitch until the team's eighth game that year.

98-54 season. The first-place Tigers featured a fifth-year player by the name of Cobb, who batted .377 that year and led the majors in home runs with nine. Who knew that when the dust settled, or at least when the sun set, that day, the two teams would have battled to a result that remains in the record books today—the longest unresolved scoreless game in the history of the American League? The closest to this performance those at the time could recall was a National League game from 1882 between the Providence Grays and the Detroit Wolverines that ended 1-0 in the eighteenth inning when Charlie "Old Hoss" Radbourn, a Providence pitcher playing right field that day for his defensive and hitting abilities, smashed a ball through an open gate in the outfield that was declared a home run.

The weather in Detroit that July 16 was not unpleasant. After an overnight low of sixty degrees, the mercury rose to a comfortable eighty-four and, most importantly, despite a shower the day before, there was no hint of rain. Bennett Field, located just west of downtown, had a capacity of 5,000 fans when it had opened in 1896 as the team's Western League home, but by the time the renamed American League claimed major league status in 1901, the stands had been extended to hold 8,500. Continued expansion brought the capacity to 14,000 by the time the park closed after the 1911 season. Players considered the playing surface dangerous because the dirt was laid over a bed of cobblestones that sometimes protruded, causing trips, bad hops, and the like.[2]

Cobblestones were not the main problem for either team on that July Friday afternoon. Rather, the problem was wood, specifically the wood in the players' bats that seemed to take an antagonistic attitude toward contact with the baseball. Through the equivalent of a doubleheader, the Tigers managed a meager six hits, the Nationals but seven. As for the line score, it is a wonder that the linotype machines at the local newspapers did not run out of zeroes. Though both teams came close to scoring several times, neither managed to do so. In all, Detroit left fifteen runners stranded and Washington nine. Washington was victimized by two unassisted double plays, one by shortstop Donie Bush and the other by first baseman Claude Rossman, but benefitted from five Detroit errors while committing only four.

In eight of the last ten innings, the Tigers had at least one base runner. Detroit had two major chances to score. The Washington starter, Dolly Gray, had given up a single to the very first batter he faced but had then held the Tigers hitless through eight innings. Sometime around the seventh inning, he injured himself—a pull or a tear was the speculation—but Gray continued pitching until throwing four pitches in the ninth, at which point he staggered and nearly fell before being helped to the clubhouse. On came Bob Groom, who entered the game facing Detroit's lead-off man, left fielder Matty McIntyre, with a 3-1 legacy count and walked him on one pitch. Bush then laid down a bunt that the Washington catcher, Gabby Street, fielded, but his throw to Jiggs Donohue at first was dropped. Sam Crawford then sacrificed to bring up Cobb, but Cobb hit a chop back to the pitcher, Groom, whose throw got McIntyre trying to score. Rossman then fanned for the third out.

The Tiger's second major opportunity came in the fifteenth. Oscar Stanage, the Detroit starting catcher, singled to center and was replaced by Red Killefer as a pinch runner. Summers bunted back to the pitcher,

Groom, who threw the ball into center field in an attempt to get the force out at second. That sent Killifer to third. Groom then walked McIntyre intentionally to create a force at the plate and a possible double play. With women screaming and dogs barking, according to one account, up came Detroit's famous "wrecking crew"—Bush, Crawford, and Cobb. Apparently, at this point, "a hysterical afternoon paper" published an Extra Edition reporting that Detroit had won the game 1-0 in fifteen innings. Alas, no. Bush fouled out to Speed Kelly at third base, bringing up the heavy-hitting Wahoo Sam Crawford. On a two-strike count, Crawford topped a roller slowly toward first. As Killifer raced down the line and slid for the plate, Groom pounced on the ball and tossed it to Street, trying for the second out at home. Street, who appeared to think the winning run had scored, headed toward the bench and the Nationals infielders also started to come in. The Detroit runners also left their bases and moved towards the club house. Even the writer from the *Washington Post* conceded that the Tigers had "undoubtedly" won the game. But home plate umpire John Kerin had judged the runner out and called everyone back onto the field to continue play. If any of the Washington infielders had made it back to their positions before the Detroiters reached their respective assigned stations, the resulting double play would have ended the inning, but that did not happen. So, play continued, and just Washington's luck, the next batter up was Cobb, who had hit two home runs, a rare feat in those times, just the day before. Cobb had already saved the game once, in the twelfth inning, when, with two out and a runner on first, Donohue, the Nationals first baseman, had hit the hardest shot of the day, a line drive headed for the right field gap, and Cobb had made a remarkable diving catch to end the threat. He also made a sensational catch in the first frame when he chased down a long foul ball along the right-field line. Now, he had a chance to nail down the victory. But Groom struck Cobb out on three pitches. The Detroit slugger had an 0-for-7 day at the plate, as did his teammate, Crawford.

Washington, too, had its chances. The best of these came in the top of the ninth when George Browne, the left fielder, led off with a walk and center fielder Clyde Milan reached on an attempted sacrifice bunt that was overrun by Rossman charging from first base. Right fielder Jack Lelivelt then failed on two bunting attempts before flying out to left.

That brought up second baseman Bob Unglaub, the cleanup hitter, who hit a popup behind first. Rossman chased it down and then managed to reach the first base bag before Milan, who had assumed the ball would fall for a hit, could get back. Another rally in the thirteenth was snuffed out when Kelly, on second after a walk and a single, tried for third base on a Summers pitch that got away from Stanage and was caught in a rundown.

It was nearly seven o'clock, and dusk was falling as the eighteenth inning ended, but the consensus in both camps was that one more inning, possibly two, could yet be played. One dissenter from the consensus, however, was Mr. Kerin, and his was the only vote that counted. He declared the game over.

If there was a hero in the game, it had to be Eddie Summers, who pitched the entire eighteen innings for the Tigers. Remarkably, he had just returned to the team from Mt. Clemens, a spa town in Michigan known in the day as "Bath City" for its health-giving mineral baths, where he was being treated for a bad knee and a "general lapse in condition," as one newspaper put it. Indeed, when the game was called for darkness, Summers himself may have lodged the loudest objection. He wanted to keep going.

The record-setting game was completed in three hours and fifteen minutes. It drew a crowd of only 3,000 or so fans, but all were entertained, if frustrated, by what they had witnessed. As one long-time Detroit booster, Sam Thompson, put it as he made his way out of the gate, "I never saw anything like it."

THE THRILL UP ON THE HILL

IF THE CONTEST in Detroit that had made way for the inaugural congressional game had been interminably scoreless, the same could not be said of that first lawmakers' standoff back in the Nationals' home park. By the time that one had ended, forty-two runs had crossed home plate, a total that was tied in an equally but opposite one-sided contest in 2024 and exceeded only once, in 1917, when forty-three runs were plated in a one-run thriller.

Anticipation was high as . . . well, there was anticipation in some quarters as the day of the game approached. When the *Washington Post* broke the story of the game in its July 10 edition, crediting Garner with originating the idea and issuing a challenge to Tener, it described the Democrats as having tired of "the drubbing which their Republican brethren have administered to them on the floor of the House." The public learned more details of the matchup from the *Washington Herald* the next day, Sunday the eleventh, though there was a lack of clarity as to when the game might be played—either the following day, Monday, or some other time. In the event, the contest was not held until the Friday of that week. The newspaper announced that Vice President Sherman would be the Republican umpire in what it assumed would be a bipartisan pairing. John Tener had reportedly proposed that both he and Speaker Cannon referee the game, but the Democrats insisted that in the interests of fairness, only one or the other might serve. Their own selection was left open, however, perhaps due to divisions within the party over precisely who and what was a Democrat. Some suggested Mr. Fitzgerald of Brooklyn for the role, but the Bryan Democrats, still influential in 1909, rejected him because of his earlier cooperation with the Republican Speaker in the rules dispute. "Grim Jim" Griggs of Georgia, who had accepted an appointment by the Speaker to serve on the Ways and Means Committee without the approval of the minority leader, was similarly excluded. Each team had, however, designated its coach: Representative Leonidas Livingston of Georgia, who was nearly eighty years old, for the Democrats, and Representative Nehemiah Sperry of Connecticut, who was over eighty and who had earlier been proposed as an umpire, for the Republicans. And by the time matters came to a head, both Vreeland for the GOP and Garner had ceded their claims of leadership to a pair of freshman field generals. Tener was to captain the GOP contestants, while Eugene Kinkead of New Jersey would lead the Democrats.

The rosters were also named, though these were to change before game day. The Democrats did object to Tener's participation because of his major league experience. He replied that he had once been a professional, it was true, but that he had since become "rankly amateurish." A compromise was reached in which Tener was allowed to play but not to pitch. The Democrats also objected to the participation of Tener's Pennsylvania colleague, Thomas Butler, on the grounds that he had played professionally in the mining region of Pennsylvania back in the Civil War era and had kept in practice ever since. Butler was 54 years old in 1909; he did not play in the game.

A dispute arose once again over the rostering of Mr. Fitzgerald, who was viewed by many of the Democrats as a traitor to the party for his earlier vote on amending the rules and who, like Mr. Sperry, had already been rejected as an umpire. Fitzgerald was recognized as one of the best players in the House, having been the star catcher of the team at Manhattan College in his youth. But as late as the day before the game, Mr. Garner, still acting as the Democratic captain, expected that Mr. Heflin of Alabama would be his pitcher. Knowing that, and knowing as well that Heflin was among the staunchest backers of Champ Clark, the Minority Leader who had been greatly offended by Fitzgerald's actions, Garner feared what might happen with Heflin throwing to Fitzgerald as his battery mate. He decreed that Fitzgerald could not play and could not even sit on the bench. So, Fitzgerald rode to the park on the streetcar rather than with the team, bought a twenty-five-cent bleacher ticket, and roundly roasted the players.

The plan, according to the pre-game news account, was that any ball hit over the fence would be deemed an out and the batter ordered off the field, that batters would be ruled out on any ball that was caught on the first bounce, and that walks would be granted only on five balls rather than four. When he was still under consideration for officiating the game, the Vice President had made it clear that he intended to preserve order on the field, but that, while disgruntled players would not be allowed to bad-mouth the umpire—and he planned to bring along the House Sergeant-at-Arms, Daniel Ransdell, to eject any rowdy players—they would be permitted to extend their remarks in the *Congressional Record*. Not without reason, the newspaper described the forthcoming contest as "a burlesque of the great national sport."[1]

News of the game apparently reached Boston just before play began. The evening edition of the July 16 *Boston Globe* captured both the context and some measure of overstated excitement with its headline: "Greater Issue Than the Tariff: All Washington Excited Over the Congressional Ball Game." The story, which featured large photos of John Tener for the Republicans and Massachusetts Congressman Joseph F. McConnell for the Democrats, continued:

> The conference on the tariff, the urgent deficiency bill [today, we would call this a supplemental appropriation], and in fact all other legislation has been forgotten. Plastered all over the lobby, back of the speaker's desk and in the cloak rooms are big notices that the game will be pulled off today. It is a rare event indeed when the sacred precincts of the house contain a notice of anything except to keep off the grass or to stay out of the private elevators, but in this case all rules have been swept to the winds.

Even at that late date, the reported lineups were those that had been originally announced, though extensive changes were then made to the Republican roster, apparently at the last minute. One correct detail added by the *Globe* noted that the game would be played for the benefit of the local playgrounds association.[2]

The game did suffer one casualty before play even started. Edward Vreeland, from the Buffalo, New York, area, who had been on Tener's original roster for the GOP, was practicing for the game at the Ellipse south of the White House together with Tener, Herbert Parsons of New York, Ralph Cole of Ohio, and others when he leaped for a high fly ball with his left arm raised, missed the ball, stepped in a hole, and crashed to the ground. The congressman was severely injured, suffering a broken collar bone and a dislocated shoulder. He managed to get to his feet, put his jacket over his shoulders, and was helped to an automobile by one of his colleagues, Bird McGuire of Oklahoma, and driven to his apartments at the Dewey Hotel at Fourteenth and L Streets, NW, where he was examined by a physician and then swathed in bandages. A report on his condition in his local Buffalo newspaper stated that it was Vreeland who had initiated the game and that he was the captain of the Republican side.[3] Butler Ames of Massachusetts took Vreeland's place in the lineup.

On the day of the game, a crowd estimated at between four hundred and one thousand raucous fans filled the grandstand.[4] The discrepancy may be explained by the following passage, which, it is worth noting, once again picks up on the continuing dispute over the tariff bill.

> The first victory of the day for the free traders was won at the gate. The game was supposed to be for charity, but everybody seemed to have a pass.
>
> "This certainly is funny," said the old gatekeeper as the passes were handed in like bills dropping into the hopper of the Speaker's desk the first day of a session. "If I got a paid-for ticket, I wouldn't know where to put it."[5]

Ticket prices ranged between twenty-five and seventy-five cents, and the game reportedly raised $320 for the Washington Playgrounds Association, which would be consistent with a *paid* attendance of around four hundred spectators. As for the remainder—and possibly the majority—of the attendees who entered with free passes? Remember. This is the Congress of the United States we are talking about.

Though he had restored the long-dormant practice of presidents attending Washington's home games just three months earlier, on April

19, and the next year would begin the tradition of the nation's chief executive throwing out the season's first pitch, President Taft was on a golf course in Chevy Chase with Vice President Sherman, by then discarded as a candidate for umpire, and did not attend the inaugural congressional contest. However, Speaker Cannon was in the house, so to speak, as was General Nelson Miles. Miles was the last officer to hold the title of Commanding General of the Army; today's equivalent is Army Chief of Staff. Cannon took a seat in a box just behind home plate and swung his leg over the railing in front of him, revealing that he was wearing purple socks. He tilted his cigar at a rakish angle and invited a dozen or so photographers present to take his picture. In the words of the *New York Sun*,

> Just to show that he pays little attention to such insignificant details as members of the House, when the game began, he inquired at great length which party was at the bat and which in the field. Having been informed, he c[r]ooked his leg over the rail of the box, tilted his cigar skyward, assumed an air of cynical wisdom and proved it by keeping quiet, for he is no Sunny Jim

Figure 11. "Uncle Joe" Cannon (left), Speaker of the House, whose purple socks are not shown here. To his left is Congressman Roberts.

Sherman in the matter of knowing baseball and it did no harm to look wise and say nothing. With the Speaker were Representative Dwight, the Republican whip; Roberts of Massachusetts; Loudenslager of New Jersey; and Rodenberg of Illinois.[6]

For the record, a search has turned up no evidence that any photographer took the Speaker up on the invitation to show off his socks to an adoring public. Also in attendance: numerous members of the House, a host of dignitaries with their attendant retinues of staffers and sycophants, and, undoubtedly, a number of lobbyists eager for a chance to rub elbows with those they would influence in other arenas.[7]

Before the fun could begin, the matter of the umpires still required resolution. Since the Democrats were unable to decide among themselves on one of their number to help referee, they also demurred on any of the Republican candidates. So, it fell to two presumably neutral parties—American League Park head groundskeeper Jim O'Day, sometimes

Directing the Workers at National Park

JIM O'DAY,
Superintendent of Ball Grounds, Who Expects to Have Everything in Readiness When Nationals Return on April 1.

THE REV. JAMES A. REYNOLDS, WHOSE SILVER JUBILEE WAS CELEBRATED AT RED BANK.

Figure 12. The Umpires: Jim O'Day and Rev. James Reynolds.

known as "Red," to call balls and strikes, and Father James A. Reynolds of Red Bank, New Jersey, to monitor the base paths. O'Day, who was misidentified as Mike "Reddie" O'Day in some of the contemporaneous accounts, including that in the *New York Times*, was the long-time head groundskeeper of Washington's major league teams dating back to 1888 and the National League squad owned by the Wagner Brothers and had many friends among players, fans, and team officials alike. He was also, by some accounts, something of a ballpark "character." In a May 1910 contest with the St. Louis Browns, for example, he was good-naturedly credited in the press with "one of the best plays of the game," to wit splashing onto the field and rescuing the second base bag from drowning in a heavy downpour.[8] O'Day was a rather burly fellow who was apparently not afraid to mix it up with players or fans who got out of line. There are at least two accounts of O'Day coming to the physical defense of umpires who were being threatened, and when Cincinnati's Harry "Farmer" Vaughn leaped into the grandstand during a game in 1898 and tried to grab a baseball from the groundskeeper, whose responsibilities seem to have included guarding the supply, he "ran a very close risk of not only being put out of the grounds but of getting a speedy straight from Jim's fist, which would have put 'Arry on the hospital list."[9]

Reynolds, a Princeton native and an 1882 graduate of Seton Hall College, had been rector of St. James Roman Catholic Church in Red Bank since 1891 and had earned a reputation as a preeminent institution builder whose organizational, fundraising, and recruiting talents were nonpareil. Recognized as a gifted raconteur, Reynolds had no known connection to baseball, but in the course of his career, had met, impressed, and befriended many prominent leaders of his state. Chances are he was attending the game at the invitation of either William Hughes or Eugene Kinkead, two members of the Democrats' team, both of whom would attend Reynolds' silver jubilee celebration the following year.[10]

By game time, of course, any remaining ambiguities regarding the rosters needed to have been resolved. The roster for the "visiting" Democrats and their positions played at various times during the game included Finis Garrett of Tennessee (second base); Thomas Heflin of Alabama (left field); William Hughes of New Jersey (first base); James McDermott of Illinois (second base and center field); William Oldfield

Figure 13. The Democratic contestants.

of Arkansas (catcher and center field); Eugene Kinkead of New Jersey (left field, catcher, and team captain); Joe T. Robinson of Arkansas (right field); Daniel Driscoll of New York (shortstop and third base); Joseph Francis O'Connell of Massachusetts (third base and shortstop); and Edwin Webb of North Carolina (pitcher).

The "home-standing" Republicans went with W. Aubrey Thomas of Ohio (third base); Ralph Cole of Ohio (right field); Albert Foster Dawson of Iowa (second base); John Tener of Pennsylvania (shortstop and actual or de facto team captain); Leonard Paul Howland of Ohio (first base); Butler Ames of Massachusetts (left field); Nicholas Longworth of Ohio (center field); James Francis Burke of Pennsylvania (catcher); and Joseph Gaines of West Virginia (pitcher).

Tener's choice of catchers came down to the last minute. Burke, described in the press as the "boy orator," claimed that he was so good that he would be playing in the major leagues, except that the congressional salary of $7,500 per year was too good to turn down. The other option was Edwin Denby of Michigan, who had learned his baseball at the University of Michigan and whose advantage was that he was so bulky that any wild pitch was likely to strike some part of his body and stay nearby. As noted, Tener went with Burke, but he may have regretted the decision. Apparently, it was not just the wild pitches that escaped Burke's grasp. By the second inning, he had missed so many opportunities that

Figure 14. The Republican contestants.

one of his Democratic colleagues shouted, "For heaven's sake, Burke, come on and catch one ball, anyway!"

As noted, Edward Vreeland of New York, the expected first baseman and a claimant to the captaincy of the team, had been placed on Injured Reserve and did not attend. He had planned to do so, however, and had even ordered a cot to be placed outside the first base coaching area so he could instruct his replacement.

The players' uniforms were not exactly uniform. Some of the participants wore Washington's home whites, grays, or blues. Mr. McDermott selected a jersey bearing the emblem of the Christian Endeavor Society; Mr. Kinkead presented in a Panama hat; and Mr. Longworth, famous for his predilection for the links, arrived in a pair of checkered golf trousers tucked into long brown stockings and a silk shirt that was described in one account as a "negligee." Mr. O'Connell arrived in a suit described by one newspaper as having been stolen from a circus clown. Mr. Heflin dressed in white flannel trousers with a black silk watch fob dangling from his belt. A pregame agreement between the teams assured that Representative Ollie James, a rather stout Kentucky Democrat, which is a nice way of saying that he weighed several hundred pounds, dressed in a pair of old trousers with reinforced suspenders so as to spare either himself or the spectators any potential embarrassment. James was expected beforehand to cover first base, which he might do quite literally, and in that event, Republicans were expected to have John Dalzell, Chairman of the House Rules Committee, bring forward a special rule holding that any batter who hit a grounder and touched any part of James himself before he caught the ball would be ruled safe at first. In the event, Mr. James did not actually play in the game—perhaps for the same reason. The cartoon in Figure 15, which appeared on the front page of the *Washington Herald* the day following the game, captures the flavor of the event, though it minimizes the aforementioned sartorial disparities.

With the Democrats first to the plate, Garrett led the way with a double. Hughes fanned, but McDermott hit a grounder to left, advancing Garrett to third base. Oldfield struck out, but Kinkead stroked a double, scoring Garrett, at which point the crowd turned to blame Ollie James for the run having scored, though he was not even in the game. Robinson then singled in McDermott before being caught off second for the third out. Democrats 2, Republicans 0.

Leading off for the Republicans, Thomas waved the bat at three pitches and sat down. Cole singled and stole second. Dawson put a ball into play and, after three or four errors, reached base while Cole scored. Dawson then tried to steal second, fell down in the base path, and was tagged out. Tener then hit a long drive to the outfield and stumbled his way to first. Howland singled, advancing Tener, and Ames did the same, driving in the second run. Longworth whiffed. Democrats 2, Republicans 2.

SOME OF THOSE SEEN IN THE BALL YARD AT THE GAME BETWEEN DEMOCRATS AND REPUBLICANS.

Figure 15. You can't tell the players without a cartoon.

Driscoll began the second inning for the Democrats but was unable to connect with any of the curve balls, estimated to travel at four miles per hour, being dished out by the GOP hurler, Mr. Gaines. O'Connell followed with a double—to shortstop—that left him standing breathless on second base. Webb's at-bat was not reported, but Garrett singled, Hughes singled, McDermott singled, Oldfield doubled and stole third, and the rout was on. Democrats 12, Republicans 2.

Burke, Gaines, and Thomas were eliminated quickly in the bottom of the inning, and the Republicans looked thoroughly disheartened. Democrats 12, Republicans 2.

The Democrats added two in the third, the Republicans one and the fourth was scoreless. Democrats 14, Republicans 3.

In the fifth inning, the Democrats were again shut out, but the Republicans rallied for their own ten-spot. Noticing that the left fielder, the "sebaceous" [fat] Mr. Heflin, together with the collie dog who had been helping him shag flies, had decided to seek shelter in the shade of a nearby tree, they began stroking hits into the sunlit area to his left. Democrats 14, Republicans 13. The game looked like it would come down to the wire.

But the Democrats were having none of that. They put five more on the scoreboard in the sixth inning and added seven more for good measure in the seventh, while the Republicans could muster only three runs in the closing frames. Final Score: Democrats 26, Republicans 16.

In general, the quality of play fell somewhere short of the ideal. As one newspaper put it, "Most of the players in trying to catch the ball held up their hands as if they expected someone to place in them very gently a salary check or a piece of pie."

There were, of course, standout performances if one interprets the term "standout" in the broadest sense. Mr. Heflin of Alabama, "playing in one of the outer gardens," was credited with one such. When the Republicans staged their big rally in the fifth, their first baseman, Mr. Howland, hit a line drive directly at Heflin, who took one look at the approaching sphere and ducked. The hit should have resulted in a home run, but when he reached second base, Howland fell to the bag exhausted and called for someone to come out and finish running for him. Separately, Nick Longworth, who thought himself a near-professional athlete, barely struck up an acquaintance with the ball, striking out twice with two runners aboard, walking once, and beating out a weak infield base hit. Finally, there was the collision. At one point during one of the Democrats' rallies, while chasing a pop fly on the infield, the GOP catcher, Burke, a slightly built man, crashed full-on into the pitcher, Gaines, who could not be described the same way, and went flying head over heels. The ball dropped unmolested while the two congressmen collected themselves and spent considerable time apologizing to one another. As they did so, three Democrats raced across the plate. In another highlight, illustrated in the upper right quadrant of the photo array in Figure 16, Mr. Burke is shown attempting to steal home as the Democrats' catcher, Mr. Oldfield, holding the ball, taunts him, yelling out, "Come to my arms, Jimmy darling." Oldfield then dropped the ball as Burke scored.

Figure 16. Game Action. Clockwise: Longworth swings for the fences; Oldfield drops the ball as Burke steals home; Robinson catches Oldfield as both score; Garrett scores on Burke's passed ball.

The Score.

DEMOCRATS.	AB.	R.	H.	PO.	A.	E.
Garrett, 2b	3	3	3	1	0	1
Heflin, lf	1	0	1	0	0	2
Hughes, 1b	6	3	2	8	1	1
McDermott, 2b., cf..	6	4	3	3	4	0
Oldfield, c., cf	6	2	3	3	1	0
Kinkead, lf., c	6	3	3	3	0	0
Robinson, rf	6	2	2	0	0	0
Driscoll, ss., 3b	4	1	0	2	1	0
O'Connell, 3b., ss.	6	5	5	1	0	1
Webb, p	5	3	3	0	2	0
Totals	49	26	25	21	9	5

REPUBLICANS.	AB.	R.	H.	PO.	A.	E.
Thomas, 3b	5	1	2	0	0	1
Cole, rf	6	3	4	0	0	1
Dawson, 2b	4	4	3	2	0	0
Tener, ss	6	3	2	2	7	1
Howland, 1b	5	2	3	7	0	2
Ames, lf	5	1	3	0	0	0
Longworth, cf	4	1	1	0	0	1
Burke, c	4	1	1	10	0	2
Gaines, p	4	0	1	0	1	1
Totals	43	16	20	21	8	9

Democrats.............. 2 10 2 0 0 5 7—26
Republicans............ 2 0 1 0 10 1 2—16

Left on bases—Democrats, 10; Republicans, 9. First base on balls—Off Webb, 3; off Gaines, 1. Struck out—By Webb, 5; by Gaines, 7. Home run—O'Connell. Two-base hits—Cole (2), Dawson, Tener, Ames, Garrett, Oldfield, Webb. Double plays—Burke (unassisted), Kinkead (unassisted). Wild pitches—Gaines, 3; Webb, 2. Passed balls—Burke, 2; Kinkead, 2. Umpires—Messrs. "Reddie" O'Day and Rev. J. A. Reynolds, Red Bank, N. J. Time of game —2 hours.

Figure 17. The Box Score of CBG1.

The box score in Figure 17 tells the tale of a game one newspaper described in a single word: Carnage. The Democrats left ten men on base while the Republicans stranded nine. There were in total only four walks, perhaps a tribute to the quality of the pitching, perhaps a tribute to the quality of the hitting—there were forty-five hits during the game—or perhaps the intended benefit of Vice President Sherman's pre-game declaration that five balls would be required for a base on balls rather than the customary four. Twelve batters struck out. Mr. O'Connell of Massachusetts was clearly the batting star, going five for six, scoring all five times, and hitting the only home run of the game and, hence, the first in congressional baseball game history. The ball did not come near to clearing a wall, but by the time it was retrieved and returned to the plate, O'Connell was—barely—able to close the final distance. He scored only because catcher Burke muffed the throw to the plate. Wags in the press suggested this was the first home run witnessed by Washington baseball fans in a very long time. But Mr. O'Day was less of a fan. On a separate occasion, when O'Connell scored from second on a passed ball, the home plate umpire sent him back to third base, and when the congressman entered an objection, he was nearly ejected from the game. Burke and Kinkead each made an unassisted double play, and Tener led all players with seven assists. Burke's double play came on a dropped third strike, which he chased halfway to first base, beating and tagging out the batter before racing back to the plate in time to tag out Mr. Driscoll, who was trying to score from third base on the play. Officially, there were fourteen errors, nine of them shared among seven different GOP players. Though a number of fly balls were hit to the outfield, no player on either team actually caught one. In the words of the *Cincinnati Enquirer*,

> The Democrats pounded the ball in much the same spirit they would hammer away at the tariff bill if "Uncle Joe" Cannon gave them half a chance, while the teamwork of the Republicans was as disjointed as their views are on the subject of raw materials and downward revision.
>
> There is only one way for the Republicans to get even, and that is through a series of special rules, which Speaker Cannon devises, containing every ingeniously cruel limitation upon the already curtailed privileges of the minority in the House. . . .
>
> The official score looked too much like a House tariff bill coming out of the Senate Committee on Finance to be printed in full.[11]

In the same vein, the Chicago *Inter Ocean* took its tongue-firmly-in-cheek shots at Speaker Cannon's use of the Rules Committee, decrying the loss of all the old traditional rules of baseball—the requirement to pitch the ball from below the hip, issuing walks on only three pitches, the ability of the batter to specify the height of the pitch to be delivered and the requirement that the batters face the pitcher at a distance of only forty-five feet.[12]

The decision to limit the game to seven innings was apparently a consensus of the moment, approved by unanimous consent rather than a plan at the outset. Among the reasons: Mr. Burke, whose exploits we have detailed, had a bump on the back of his head from his run-in with Mr. Gaines. Mr. Heflin could barely move after chasing down so many fly balls in left field. Mr. O'Connell's trousers were starting to come apart. Mr. Longworth, known to his colleagues as "Son-in-Law Long-worth" for his marriage to Teddy Roosevelt's daughter Alice, was longing for a respite at the Metropolitan Club. The newspaper reporters were expressing exhaustion at trying to keep up with things. And no one had thought to bring along a supply of anything other than sarsaparilla and some bad-tasting soda water.

At that point, the game had lasted for two hours. It is not clear how many of the players did the same. When it was over, the stouter members of the House were observed groggily huffing and puffing from their exertion on what was one of the capital's hotter days of that summer, while the leaner members were simply lying prone on the grass, too exhausted to get up. The crowd was weary as well, having worn itself out laughing. For his part, Speaker Cannon did not stick around until the conclusion. Once it became clear his minions would be defeated, Uncle Joe threw down his big black cigar and stomped out of the ballpark. Mr. Heflin took notice, shouting after him, "Hurrah for the Democratic party!" The *New York Times* took a more staid position, noting that Cannon looked "powerless to call the minority to order or bring in a special rule shutting off base hits. . . ." One unnamed member of the Democrats' team was more pointed. "We had scores to settle," he said following the game, "and this sort of partly evens things up, though I'm rather afraid that 'Uncle Joe' will plant his foot more firmly on some of our necks to get back at us."[13]

STURM UND DRANG

AS TIRED AS they were, the players had little time to lie around on the field and rest. Once the baseball gods were done with them, the weather gods took their turn.

Game day, Friday the sixteenth, was sunny, with a high of 92 degrees. It was a typical July day for the nation's capital—hazy, hot, and humid. News accounts described the conditions on the field as uncomfortably warm. And as often happens in Washington, shortly before seven in the evening, not long after the game had ended, the weather broke with the arrival of a line of thundershowers. But this was no ordinary line of showers. Official records show the total rainfall that day totaled 0.42 inches. But rainfall totals in the area often vary quite widely, and the conditions in the vicinity of mid-Atlantic thunderstorms can be quite localized. The German literary term *"Sturm und Drang"* generally refers to conditions of rousing action, high emotionalism, and stress. In this case, the *Sturm* was quite literal. The *Drang* was perhaps more figurative, but we will get to that in a moment.

The headline on the front page of the *Washington Herald* the next morning—the same front page that included stories on both the congressional game and the Nationals-Tigers one-game doubleheader—read, "Lightning Strikes Washington Homes: Freak Storm Wreaks Damage in Center of City." The heart of the storm struck first along the waterfront across the Potomac from the direction of Alexandria, Virginia, then cut a northerly swath through the southwest quadrant of the city to the area of Judiciary Square, the site in 1909 of the United States District Court for the District of Columbia and the D.C. Court of Appeals, which is located between the Capitol Building and the White House. That is where it seems to have done the most damage. Three houses along New Jersey Avenue, NW, were struck by lightning, which tore away brick, windowsills, skylights, and chimneys and lifted off roofs. The greatest tree damage was mainly at Judiciary Square and the parking area around the nearby Pension Office Building, where huge trees that were several feet thick at the base were pulled from the ground and swept along like twigs. Limbs were ripped off and blown around, and shrubs were beaten by the rain and uprooted. An estimated five hundred trees were destroyed in an area roughly bounded by Pennsylvania Avenue, K Street, New Jersey Avenue, and Fifth Street, all in the city's northwest quadrant, with more damage in the southwest nearer the point of origin. Many streets ran like rivers from curb to curb, and many remained blocked with debris until the following day or beyond. More giant old trees were lost on the National Mall, and the Mall itself was flooded. Rainfall was heavy to the northwest and southeast of the storm's main track, but the wind damage was inconsequential in those areas. The anemometer on the weather bureau building at Twenty-Fourth and M Streets, NW, registered a top gust of only twenty-five miles per hour—not nearly enough to cause such severe damage. Large crowds of baseball fans—not those at American League Park, but rather those who had gathered outside the newspaper buildings downtown to follow the seemingly endless contest in Detroit—ran for cover when the storm struck. Several horses broke and ran out of fear, but although one horse-drawn mail wagon collided with a streetcar, all of the steeds were stopped either by their drivers or by pedestrians and damage or injuries to persons were averted. And then it was over as quickly as it began. The rain stopped, the sun came out, and the temperature became delightfully cool.[1]

The map in Figure 18 can be used to locate the path of the storm and the area of primary damage. The docks of the waterfront are visible along the Washington Channel at the lower right. The heart of the storm then traveled straight upward to Judiciary Square at the center of the map, where it seems to have dissipated. The White House and the Ellipse (termed here the Executive Grounds) are down from the square and to the left; the Capitol is down and to the right. For reference, at the top

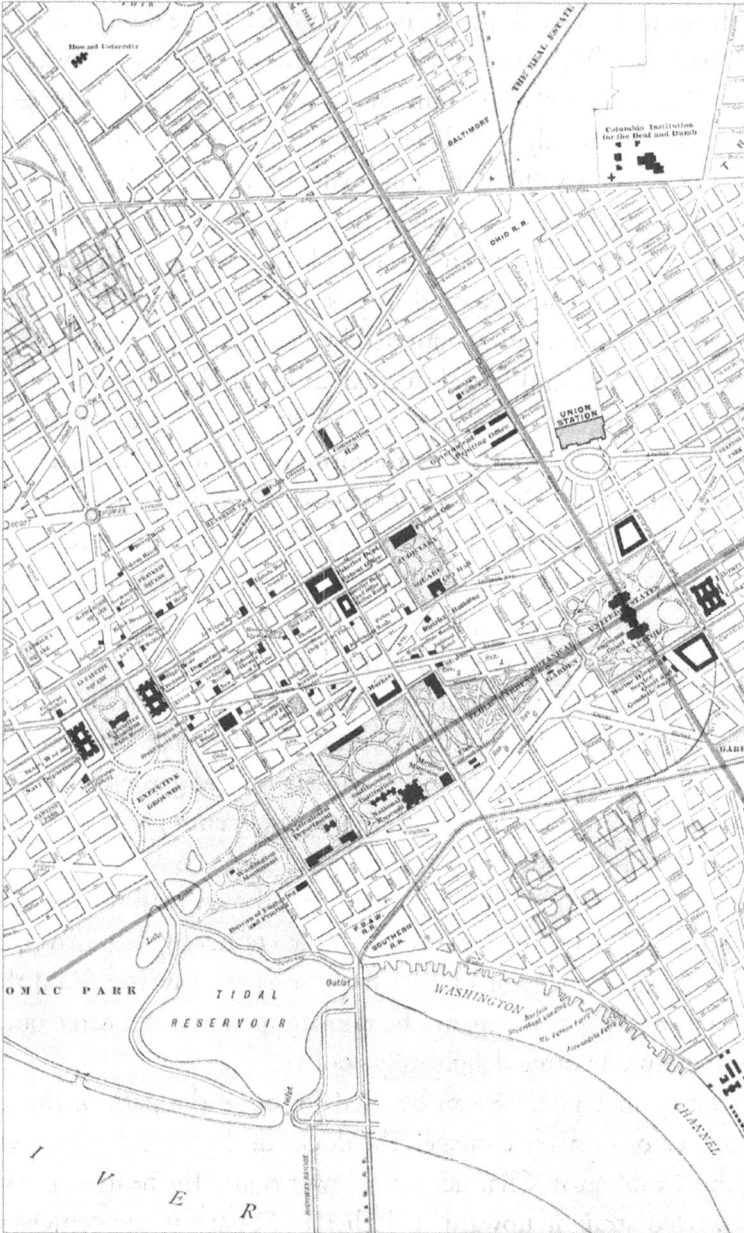

Figure 18. Map of the area affected by the freak storm of July 16, 1909.

left-hand corner of the map is a building labeled Howard University. Just below that is a large open plot with a peninsular extension at its lower left. That is where American League Park was located.

One place that barely escaped the storm was Fort Myer, across the Potomac from the Washington waterfront, where a large crowd had gathered to witness a demonstration flight by Orville Wright, who was attempting to interest the military in purchasing aeroplanes. Wright's plane had been placed on a monorail earlier in the afternoon in preparation for the flight, but when the wind kicked up and light rain began to fall, the machine was returned to its shed and the demonstration was put off until the following day. By the time the weather had cleared and the winds calmed, the Wrights and the military assistants and observers had gone to dinner.[2] In the meantime, the Wright brothers' principal competitor for the military contract, Glen Curtiss, completed a successful demonstration flight that lasted twenty-five to thirty minutes, depending on the observer. But Curtiss had an advantage: His flight was not in the Washington area but over the Hempstead Plains on Long Island.[3]

Another place that seems to have escaped the storm altogether was the building occupied by the *Washington Post*. The next morning's edition of the paper reported that a large crowd of fans had gathered to watch the big scoreboard carrying news of the Nationals-Tigers matchup in Detroit and that it still numbered about two thousand people when the game was called off long after seven o'clock. But the only stories the paper carried about the storm that had devastated the city the night before included one long feature on the delayed Wright brothers' flight and a brief writeup about a coal and lumber dealer in Alexandria who had been using the telephone when there was a bolt of lightning from a relatively clear sky. The man was stunned briefly and suffered a slight burn on his neck and left forearm; his conversation was briefly interrupted.[4] At the time, the newspaper was headquartered on E Street, NW, between Thirteenth and Fourteenth Streets, directly west of Judiciary Square. If the published account of scoreboard watching was correct, this marks just how narrow the path was that the storm cut through the center of the city. It is certainly within the realm of possibility that the storm missed the *Washington Post*. The question is, however, how did the *Washington Post* miss the storm?

Today, we might look for evidence that the "freak" storm of July 16 was either a tornado or a derecho—a storm with powerful, highly localized downdrafts. Both are somewhat common in the area. At the time, the damage was compared to that of a tropical typhoon or a mini cyclone, but the storm itself was not labeled as such.

So much for the *Sturm*. As for the *Drang*, let us consider the condition of the participants in the game on the following morning. If not under stress, per se, it seems that all of them were, at the very least, in some form of *distress*. Or so the wags at the *Washington Herald* would have had their readers believe. "List of Cripples Numbers Twenty: All the

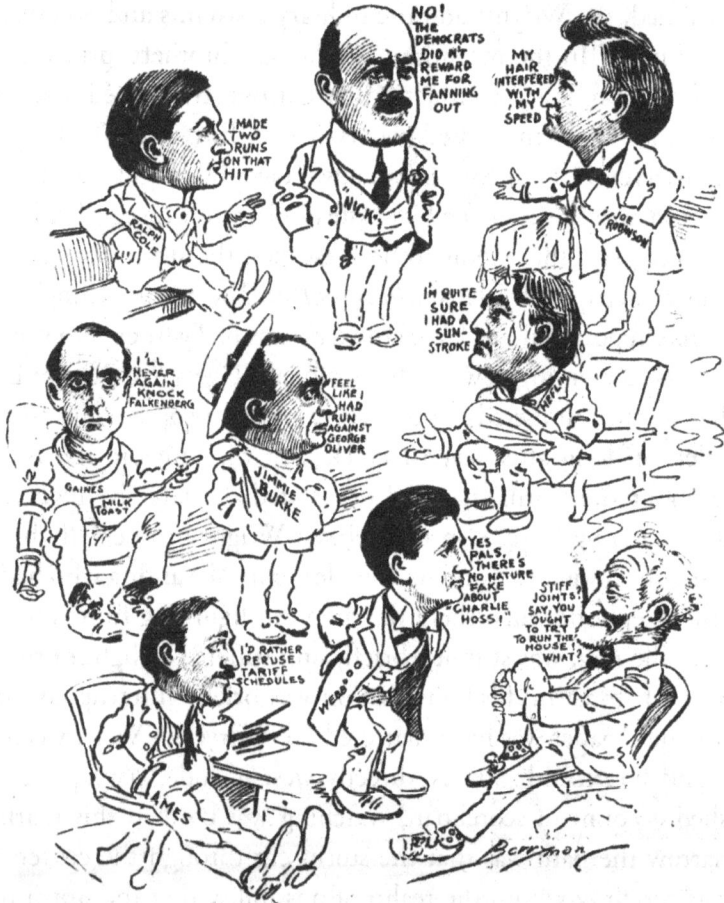

Figure 19. The Survivors.

Bruises Science Knows," read the morning-after headline, the number of sufferers exceeding by one the number of participants in the game. Mr. Burke was said to be sore in his *quadratus lumborum* [a deep backache], while battery mate Gaines claimed an outrageous pain in his *flexor longus pollicis* [a sore arm]. Webb, the Democrats' hurler, suffered from twinges of the *flexor minimi digiti* [a stiff little finger]. Cole was said to be experiencing paralysis of the *obicularis oris* [the muscle surrounding the mouth] because of his many but, fortunately, unsuccessful efforts to catch high popups in his mouth. And the man who served Joe Robinson's breakfast reported that his *pronator radii teres* [a muscle of the forearm] exploded like a pistol shot when he tried to lift a glass of water to take a sip. Even Tener was suffering, said the newspaper, having strained his *gastrocnemius* and *tibialis anticus* [leg muscles] chasing ground balls that often remained out of reach. The newspaper concluded that the real winners were not the Democrats with their twenty-six runs, but rather "the physicians, the druggists, the masseurs, the Turkish baths, and the arnica manufacturers" whose services and products would benefit from the attentions being paid to the "muscles, the ligaments, the tendons, and the sinews of the wounded."[5] The *Washington Evening Star* may have captured the post-game moment most succinctly with the front-page cartoon in Figure 19.

PAST AS PROLOGUE:
LIFE AFTER CBG 1

JULY 16, 1909, was an extraordinarily eventful day for Washingtonians. The Nationals and the Detroit Tigers played an eighteen-inning scoreless marathon, followed by thousands on downtown newspaper scoreboards, which remains in the record books to this day. The Republicans and Democrats in the House of Representatives squared off in the very first congressional baseball game. A freak storm caused damage and a massive loss of mature trees as it etched a path through the very heart of the city, barely missing both the White House and the Capitol Building. Even Wilbur and Orville Wright couldn't escape the drama as they were forced to postpone an important demonstration of their aeroplane for the U.S. Army just across the river at Fort Myer, Virginia. We have already looked backward from that day to examine some of the personalities, trends, and forces that provided context for CBG1. And we have looked at the game itself from all angles. Now, the time has come to rotate our lens toward the future and trace the paths of some of these same personalities, trends, and forces in the days and years that followed.

A good place to begin is with some of the characters who appear in our drama but not as players in the ballgame. Pride of place would naturally go to the Speaker of the House, **Joseph Gurney "Uncle Joe" Cannon**. If any one individual drove the full range of the action in our story, it would be him. Cannon came into our story at the peak of his power, and he applied that power in full measure, working closely and cynically with Nelson Aldrich and Sereno Payne to mask his intent and literally shutting down the House until he had his way with the tariff bill. But afterward he watched that power dissipate. At the beginning of the Second Session of the Sixty-First Congress, on March 17, 1910, a coalition of Democrats and Republican rebels led by progressive Republican George Norris of Nebraska came together to make fundamental changes in the makeup of the Rules Committee, depriving the Speaker of the ability to name members of that powerful committee or to serve on it himself. They waited to introduce their measure until Saint Patrick's Day, when many regular Republicans were absent from the House celebrating in the streets of Washington, and it was only after two days of delays, power plays, and debate that it came to a vote.[1] Their resolution, which passed 191-156 on March 19 after a great deal of parliamentary wrangling and an explicit repudiation of the Speaker, read as follows:

Resolved, That the rules of the House be amended as follows:

> The Committee on Rules shall consist of 15 members, 9 of whom shall be members of the majority party and 6 of whom shall be members of the minority party, to be selected as follows:
> The States of the Union shall be divided by a committee of three, elected by the House for that purpose, into nine groups, each group containing, as near as may be, an equal number of Members belonging to the majority party. The States of the Union shall likewise be divided into six groups, each group containing, as near as may be, an equal number of Members belonging to the minority party.
> At 10 o'clock a.m. on the day following the adoption of the report of said committee, each of said groups shall meet and select one of its number a member of the Committee on Rules. . . .
> The Committee on Rules shall select its own chairman.
> The Speaker shall not be eligible to membership on said committee.
> All rules or parts thereof inconsistent with the foregoing resolution are hereby repealed.[2]

Boom! That is what is known in politics as a beatdown, and despite some claw backs in later years, it altered the power of the Speaker of the

House to this day. And no sooner had that reform passed than Representative Charles Fowler of New Jersey, who had been deposed as chair of the Committee on Banking and Currency by Speaker Cannon, presumably to clear the position for Mr. Vreeland, tried to take advantage of a day with minimal attendance to impose further restrictions on the naming of committee members, though he was stopped by the adept parliamentary maneuvering of Mr. Payne.[3]

The conclusion one must draw is that CBG1 may have defused somewhat the ill feelings among members in the short term and helped smooth passage of the final version of Payne-Aldrich, but if so it was a mere band-aid laid over the tensions in the House that was ripped from the wound at the earliest available moment. And that was not the end of the matter. Later that year, in the 1910 elections, Republicans lost their majority in the House and, as a direct consequence, Cannon lost his speakership and the balance of his powers. He remained in the House until 1923, and when he retired he was portrayed on the cover of the very first issue of *Time Magazine*.[4] A decade later, he was honored when the first House office building, which had been necessitated when the body outgrew its quarters in the Capitol and had been built during his years as Speaker, known until then as the Old House Office Building, was renamed in his honor. But after 1909, his influence was never the same.

Sereno Payne was first elected to Congress in 1882, and by 1909 was serving as both Majority Leader and Chairman of the Ways and Means Committee, in which positions he continued through the end of the Sixty-First Congress in 1910. Payne remained in Congress as a member of the minority through the Sixty-Third Congress. He was elected to another term in 1914 but died in December of that year before the new Congress convened.

If Messrs. Cannon and Payne were disadvantaged by the outcome of the 1910 elections, quite the opposite was true of **John J. Fitzgerald**. Recall that it was Fitzgerald who had angered his Democratic colleagues by voting with Cannon on the adoption of rules in 1909. He had been rewarded by Cannon with a position on the Rules Committee but banned by his party from participating in any way in the initial congressional ballgame. Apparently, all was forgiven after the Democrats gained control of the House. Fitzgerald was named to chair the Appropriations

Committee under the new regime, a position he held until he retired from Congress in 1917.

While we are focused on politicians, let us not forget **President Taft**. Though he hovered in the background for much of our tale, in the end he won congressional passage of the income tax amendment, but having failed at the very outset of his term to depose Speaker Cannon and advance the cause of the progressive wing of his party, he was unable to carry the day on tariff reductions. His Republican predecessor, Teddy Roosevelt, took this as a personal afront, enough of one that he entered the 1912 presidential campaign as a third-party contender. Roosevelt lost the election, but he split the Republican vote and thus deprived Taft of four additional years in the White House. In some measure, then, Cannon's, Payne's, and Aldrich's hardnosed protectionism and cynical strategizing paved the way for Woodrow Wilson's election in 1912.

And what of the two self-identified team captains and possible originators of CBG1? The Democrat, **John Nance Garner**, rose through the ranks and served as Speaker of the House from December 1931 until February 1933, then as Vice President of the United States during Franklin Roosevelt's first two terms, 1933-1941. Today he is perhaps best

Figure 20. Roosevelt plays the spoiler.

known for his supposed characterization of the latter office as "not worth a bucket of warm spit."[5] For his part, though he lost his chairmanship of the banking committee when the GOP lost control of the House after the 1910 elections, **Edward Vreeland**, who was a pregame factor in both the Baltimore trip and CBG1, continued in Congress until 1913.

That brings us to the umpires. As we noted, **Father James A. Reynolds**, a prominent New Jersey clergyman, celebrated his silver jubilee in the priesthood in 1910. A mark of his prominence in the state is found in the guest list, which, in addition to the congressmen noted above, included New Jersey Governor Edward Stokes, Senators Frank Briggs and John Kean, and Congressman Benjamin Franklin Howell.[6] Unfortunately, Reynolds was stricken with the liver ailment known at the time as dropsy (and today as edema) and died following surgery in May 1914. He was held in such high regard that a special funeral train was commissioned to carry his remains from Red Bank to Princeton for burial.[7]

Jim "Red" O'Day's life after CBG1 was not without its own tragic ending but also had its routine challenges and special successes. Throughout, it was woven into the fabric of American League Park. By 1911 (the precise date is uncertain), O'Day had been promoted to Superintendent of Ball Grounds, which brought under his purview not just the grounds but the stadium itself. March of 1911 found him overseeing a major remodel of the facility that would add five hundred new seats and construct a series of new entrances to facilitate access for the fans. As described in the *Washington Times* of March 13,

> There will be a half dozen entrance ways on the west side. Two will be for grandstand patrons, three for those who watch the games from the [new] pavilion, and the old one for the bleacherites.
>
> Instead of the old system of buying the tickets and then turning to the right the new gates are built in such a manner that one may buy a coupon in passing the ticket sellers and then continue straight in through the stiles, which are but five yards beyond the box offices.
>
> The old incline to the grandstand has been completely done away with, and in its place has been built a modern chute, six feet wider than the abandoned one. . . . To the right of the top of this

incline is the umpires' room, and to the left a new refreshment booth.

The lavatory accommodations have been trebled, and all plumbing, including that in the clubhouse, is to be most modern. For the women a special retiring room is being built to the northern side of the big stand.

At the extreme northeastern end of the left field is to be built a pavilion which will accommodate 500 more fans and under this will be a space through which automobiles may pass to be banked behind the grandstand and pavilion.[8]

A grand plan indeed, and apparently the end of the provision of space for fans to tie up their horses.

But remember, this was Washington. So, it should not be surprising that the headline in the same newspaper a mere four days later told a different tale: "Grandstand and Bleachers Go in Mysterious Fire At Ball Grounds." Remember that Shakespeare stanza? The blaze was discovered at noon on Friday, the seventeenth, as it swept through the dry tiers of bleacher seats in right field, fanned by strong winds. O'Day was having a conversation with a bicycle policeman and Joe Dondero, who served as umpire and referee in many local semi-pro athletic contests, when the group noticed a curl of smoke. O'Day then tried to put the fire out himself with his hands, but was burned around his left wrist, and by the time the policeman had reached a call box and the firemen had responded and connected their first pipeline, the grandstand and most of the remaining structure was a total loss. After just half an hour, only the clubhouse in the northeast corner and a portion of the left field bleachers were saved. The fire had also leaped to the original wooden building that had housed the Freedmen's Hospital and was now used as a storage building for the adjacent Eisinger Lumber Yard, and that was lost. The firemen turned their attention to saving the lumber yard itself, which they were able to do. The yard had burned twice in the preceding four years, it seemed, each instance suspected of being arson, but no cause was evident for the fire starting at the adjacent ballpark. There was electrical wiring under the area where it apparently started, but because of the construction the wires were not live. And at the time no one other than the three conferees was known to be in the park.[9]

The Nationals were scheduled to play their first home game of the season on April 12, which left mere weeks to recreate a functioning ballpark. The alternatives were to play early season games at Union League Field or to move those games to Boston or New York. There was no time to waste, and within four days, on Tuesday, March 21, the following classified advertisement appeared:

WILLIAM GIFFORD
Professional Building Wrecker

Fire wood to anyone who will haul it away. Come quick. Monday morning will be cleared away by 10 o'clock for the new stands to be put up. American League Park, Seventh St. at Florida Ave.[10]

By April 2, the reconstruction of the stands by the Fuller Construction Company was well underway, with 800 men working around the clock, aided at night by huge electric lights. In some places, old wooden floors were being replaced by concrete, and the location of the field was being adjusted slightly. By April 9, the team was sufficiently confident of the completion of the rebuild that they began to sell box seats for Opening

Preparing Playing Field and Removing Lumber From New Stands at National Park for Opening Game Season With Boston Red Sox.

Figure 21. Preparing the field, removing lumber from the stands, April 8, 1911.

Day. They also opened the park to fans for a look at the progress, and between five and ten thousand showed up.[11] Given the condition of the facility the day before, as shown in the photo in Figure 21, that seemed a touch optimistic.

But they made it! The park, soon to be renamed as Griffith Stadium, opened on schedule on April 12. And once inside, fans found little resemblance to the old ballpark—the center field fence, the clubhouse, and one set of bleacher seats. When finished—and there was still work to do—the new cement amphitheater would seat fourteen thousand spectators. Mr. O'Day must have breathed a sigh of relief. Figure 22 shows the scene as fans waited for the gates to open.[12] Among the changes that year designed to improve the spectating experience was one more. Managing owner Clark Griffith decided that in 1912 the team would open sales offices in downtown Washington where fans could purchase their ducats in advance, thereby avoiding altogether the lines at the ballpark, a convenience already offered by every other major league club.[13]

The following year O'Day got some serious help when Griffith hired Frederick Fitzgerald to serve as the new groundskeeper under

Figure 22. The rebuilt National Park, Opening Day 1911.

the superintendent. Fitzgerald came to Washington from Philadelphia, where he had been in charge of the National League grounds.[14] And aside from some special projects, such as preparing the park for World Series play, matters continued on a more or less routine basis until 1926.

On January 3, 1926, work was begun on remodeling the stadium once again and replacing the grass with new sod. The football season had run later than usual, and the field was in poor condition, so farm equipment was brought in for the major makeover. But just as everything was torn up in preparation for resodding, the weather turned cold, threatening to shorten the time available for the new grass to establish itself.[15] The pressure on O'Day must have been intense, for just a few days later he suffered a heart attack that forced his retirement. Having spent thirty-eight of his fifty-eight years working for the Washington baseball club in its various incarnations, Jim O'Day passed away on November 14, 1926.[16]

As for **the Nationals, cum Senators**, well, they finished the 1909 season with forty-two wins and a hundred ten losses, fifty-six games out of first place in the American League. Along the way, they set American League records for the fewest runs scored in a season (380) and the most shutout losses (29). The team managed winning records in six of the next fourteen seasons, led by a pitcher who had joined the team in 1907, and in his first three seasons went 5-9, 14-14, and 13-25. In a 1909 game against the New York Highlanders, for example, a 19-0 loss, this Washington starter was described in the press as failing to improve and going to pieces.[17] Then Walter Johnson figured it out. From 1910 through 1919, Johnson never had a losing season and never won fewer than twenty games, topping out with a record of 36-7 in 1913. He returned to form in 1924 and carried the team to its first and only World Series win, earning his second American League Most Valuable Player award in the process, and eventually earning inclusion in the very first cohort of five players selected for induction into the National Baseball Hall of Fame. The Senators moved to Minnesota in 1961.

That brings us to the three main elements of our story—the tariff bill, John Tener, and, of course, the congressional baseball game.

When we last left **the tariff**, it passed the House in April and was sent to the Senate, where it was referred to Nelson Aldrich's Finance Committee. There it was amended more than eight hundred times and reshaped into a far more protectionist form and was packaged with a two percent tax on the incomes of large corporations to make it more palatable to progressive interests. Then, around the time of the Payne-Tener visit to Baltimore, President Taft sent a message to Congress proposing a constitutional amendment to allow the imposition of a personal income tax— in effect, a deceptive signal, again to the progressives, that the reductions they anticipated in the new tariff bill would necessitate a new income stream for the federal government. And there things stood in late June.

Moving with unaccustomed alacrity, by July 12 the proposed income tax amendment had passed both the House and the Senate and been sent to the states for ratification. The progressives were pleased, but Cannon and the conservative Republicans were satisfied as well. As we noted, they saw the amendment as a sham, a bright shiny object to distract the reformers. They were confident that it would never be ratified by enough states to come into effect. In the meantime, nothing else was moving through the House of Representatives for the simple reason that there were no committees to process and advance legislation. The pressure built. Think of a parent in the midst of a string of dangerously hot summer days. The kids are cooped up inside. They've run out of things to do. It's getting ugly. Any parent in that situation would arrive at the same conclusion that Speaker Cannon, Majority Leader Payne, and quite possibly Chairman Vreeland did. We need to get the kids out of the House. *Voilà, c'est ça.* How about a baseball game? And on July 16, that is precisely what they staged. They bought some time, and then things started to move. Let's pick up the tick-tock from there.

DATE	DAY	ACTION
JUL 17	125	
JUL 18	126	
JUL 19	127	
JUL 20	128	
JUL 21	129	
JUL 22	130	
JUL 23	131	
JUL 24	132	

DATE	DAY	ACTION
JUL 25	133	
JUL 26	134	
JUL 27	135	
JUL 28	136	
JUL 29	137	
JUL 30	138	The conference report is presented to the House
JUL 31	139	After very limited debate, the House approves the conference report (passes the Payne-Aldrich Tariff Act) by a vote of 195-183 with 10 not voting
AUG 1	140	
AUG 2	141	
AUG 3	142	
AUG 4	143	
AUG 5	144	The Senate passes the conference report by a vote of 70-22; President Taft signs the bill into law; **Speaker Cannon appoints members to all of the sixty or so customary standing committees; the Special Session of Congress adjourns.** The House will not reconvene until December.

In the final days of discussion in the conference committee, Taft and others were staking out positions in public while representatives of various interests were hashing out the final details behind closed doors—and leaking word of their efforts, if only to assuage their own supporters. The newspapers were filled with highly detailed accounts.[18] Then after some parliamentary maneuvering that further inflamed the Democrats and the progressives, who discovered that they were being afforded no opportunity to amend the final version of the bill once it had come back from the Senate, and further, that the bill was on balance no longer one of reform but instead extended the protectionist tariffs, on July 31 the House passed the conference report on Payne-Aldrich by a margin of twelve votes with ten abstentions, and on August 5, the Senate did the same.[19]

The *Congressional Record* for that day shows that, literally within minutes of being informed of Senate passage, Speaker Cannon relented and appointed Members to all of the customary committees, though he extracted one last pound of flesh by replacing three insurgent Republican committee chairs with members who had been loyal to him on the tariff.[20] The relevant page is shown in Figure 23.[21]

We have already seen what happened to Speaker Cannon at the beginning of the following session of the Sixty-First Congress. He lost many of his most important powers. We saw, too, what happened to the Republicans in the elections that following year. They lost control of the

Figure 23. Page of the *Congressional Record* from August 5, 1909.

House. And we saw what happened to President Taft when he next came before the voters in 1912. Teddy Roosevelt took him out. All of this was, in large measure, a product of the 1909 tariff reform battle. But what of the proposed income tax amendment? And what of the tariff?

Much to the surprise of the conservatives in the House, the Sixteenth Amendment was ratified by the last required state on February 3, 1913, thereby authorizing Congress to impose a tax on individual incomes. Not of a mind to miss such an opportunity, Congress then proceeded to enact a progressive levy with a top marginal tax rate of six percent on incomes over half a million dollars. As for the Payne-Aldrich tariff schedule? In that same year, 1913, Congress passed yet another tariff bill, one that substantially reduced the protectionist duties on many hundreds of goods, from abrasives to zinc. As an indicator of the extent of the changes, in 1918, the American Protective Tariff League published a book, *Protective Tariff Cyclopedia (revised)*, that listed every specific duty on every product under both Payne-Aldrich and the 1913 law known as the Underwood Act. In print that is barely large enough to read, the list covers one hundred forty-seven pages.[22]

Put another way, the entire protectionist gambit failed. It failed in slow motion, to be sure, but it failed spectacularly.

We have spent some time suggesting what **John Tener** was not. He was not a diligent or influential Member of Congress. In fact, he was barely there, either in length of service or in attendance. And it is at least reasonable to argue that he was not the person who came up with the initial idea for the first congressional baseball game. Chances are that Messrs. Cannon, Payne, Vreeland, and perhaps even Garner played roles in that enterprise. In that regard, it is worth noting that *both* team captains—Tener and Eugene Kinkead—were first-term congressmen. Arguably, the task of organizing a team to compete for one's party is precisely the kind of low-level responsibility that more senior members might assign to such freshmen.

Tener certainly made an important contribution, but it seems creditable, even likely, that he was recruited to the task. Indeed, it may well be the case that, even as he was asked to arrange the visit of the delegation of congressmen and lobbyists to Baltimore in June, one purpose of that trip might have been for Payne or Vreeland to ask Tener to help arrange the subsequent congressional game. It is worth remembering that Vreeland was Chair of the Banking Committee and Tener was still a bank president, a position he had not relinquished, so the two certainly might have been acquainted before he arrived in Congress, or Tener may have sought out Vreeland upon his arrival to highlight their common interest. As the proximate agent of the Republican leadership, Tener did take the lead in organizing the GOP *team*, though as noted, his roster was never really set until the very last moment and included almost none of the colleagues he had initially named. Plus, as we suggested earlier, organizing the team is a far different and more limited task than organizing the *game*.

Even as one account suggested that he was the prime mover behind the game and the one who challenged John Garner rather than the reverse, a United Press writeup that appeared in the *Pittsburgh Press*, a hometown newspaper for the congressman from western Pennsylvania, seemed to suggest that it was a last-minute affair.[23] Tener's reputation as a former major league pitcher certainly helped to fuel interest in the contest, both in the House and in the larger community, which is to say the press. But, given the success of the game in drawing partisans together and reducing tensions on the Hill, if Tener had provided the impetus in 1909 and that had enhanced his reputation or influence on the Hill, what would have prevented him from doing the same in 1910, the second year of his term? One might argue that he was distracted by his impending gubernatorial campaign, but set against that must be the extensive and entirely favorable publicity that Tener, in particular, received attendant on the 1909 contest and that he might expect to receive again in 1910. So, a second game might have been expected to enhance further his public persona going into the Pennsylvania race. Yet there was no game, nor any apparent consideration of holding one, the following year. President Taft was left to decide whether to root for the Chamber of Commerce or the all-newspaper team in the year's main charity contest at American League Park on June 22, that one for the benefit of the Society for the Prevention of Tuberculosis.[24]

All of that said, neither politics nor baseball was through with John Tener at that point. In some ways, he was just getting started. In 1910, Tener was renominated by the GOP for his congressional seat and then later nominated as the party's candidate for Governor of Pennsylvania.

On July 26, he formally withdrew from the congressional race, but after winning the 1910 gubernatorial election, he held fast to his congressional seat until the very eve of his inauguration as Governor in January 1911.[25]

Tener notched several accomplishments as Governor, including passage of the first state school code, creation of the state's Public Service Commission to regulate utilities, building of a reformatory for women and two tuberculosis hospitals, enactment of a soft coal mining code, creation of a state board of education and a state labor and industry department, and the nation's first Board of Motion Picture Censors, the latter a dubious accomplishment by modern lights. He also made substantial improvements to the state's roads and led in framing model game conservation laws, flood control projects, and workmen's compensation programs.[26] But for our purposes, his most interesting undertaking may have been the campaign he began in 1912 to do away with baseball gambling pools, an effort that had national reach and garnered national attention.

Tener had become convinced that rampant gambling on such aspects as high scores, inning-specific outcomes, and game results that was taking place in cafes, hotels, stores and on the streets put baseball in danger of being spoiled. As he put it, "Baseball has won its great place in the affections of the American people because it has been clean . . . I would be mighty sorry to see it fall, and I sincerely hope those who can will help stamp out betting on the games. It is the greatest danger baseball has to-day."[27] Within a week, the Governor's statement had reportedly led to favorable commentary across the country, as well as commitments of support from some local district attorneys whose view seemed to be that no new laws were needed to achieve this objective, only a willingness to enforce those already in place.[28] Apparently, much of the problem originated in Pennsylvania, and more specifically, with the *Wilkes-Barre Weekly World* newspaper, which offered prizes to the winners of pools operated by the paper for those who purchased copies, many of them residing far from the Commonwealth. Much of the detail emerged in the 1915 trial of a Chicago news dealer who had been charged with gambling offenses based on his selling of the newspaper. In the words of the prosecutor, "The newspaper feature is only a blind. More than 40,000 persons have paid 30 cents for the chance at the prizes. If this sort of thing is permitted to continue, base ball will share the disrepute which gambling brought to prize fighting and horse racing."[29] If that strikes readers as prescient given the World Series scandal just four years later, they would not be alone.

While Governor, whenever he would visit Philadelphia, Tener made a point of touching base with his long-time friend William F. Baker, president of the Phillies. So, it would not be surprising to learn that Baker was paying close attention when Tener began his crusade against gambling on the game. By 1913, shortly after the campaign had begun in earnest, there was growing dissatisfaction among the owners with the performance of National League president Thomas Lynch. Four of their number—Garry Herrmann of Cincinnati, Barney Dreyfus of Pittsburgh, Charles Ebbets of Brooklyn, and Schuyler Britton of St. Louis—had reached out to Bob Brown, editor of the *Louisville Times*, to serve as a possible replacement for Lynch, but the group had been unable to muster another vote to achieve a majority of the eight owners. That's when Baker stepped in and said he would back Lynch for another year unless a stronger alternative could be found. Goodness, he said, I'd bet John Tener would do it.

Not quite so fast. It turned out that Brown, the newspaper editor, was a close friend of Tener's and that the two had something special in common—each had served as Grand Exalted Ruler of the Elks. Tener indicated he would not accept the job if Brown were also under consideration. This led Hermann and Dreyfus to withdraw their support for Brown, which eventually resulted in the naming of Tener to the post. The vote was taken on December 9, 1913.[30] But Tener did not come without conditions, the principal one of which was that he would hold both jobs—Governor of Pennsylvania *and* President of the National League—until his gubernatorial term expired in January 1915. He also demanded that he receive a multi-year contract (he got four years) and that the salary for the position be raised from the then-current ten thousand dollars per year to twenty-five thousand, matching the pay of American League president Ban Johnson. Tener agreed that he would not double-dip and would not accept his new salary until his term as Governor had ended. An arrangement was worked out for that first year in which John Heydler, the secretary-treasurer of the league, would handle the routine business while Tener would handle the higher-order items and represent the league on the National Commission.[31]

Lynch, who was being unceremoniously replaced, had the last word: "In choosing your next president, gentlemen, you have gone on record as wanting a man who will lend dignity and prestige to the National League. In your election of Governor Tener for the position, you have the right man. I hope you will inject some of that dignity expected of him into yourselves . . ."[32]

Though it would not have been understood as such at the time, we can see with hindsight that bringing in Tener, an active foe of gambling, was a harbinger of the later hiring and empowering of Kenesaw Mountain Landis as the first Commissioner of Baseball to rid the game of the same scourge. In that, obviously, Tener was not successful. But he brought other strengths to the job, not least, given his participation in the Players League in 1890, an understanding of the mindset of the players, an understanding that would serve him well in the challenge that was soon to be mounted by the upstart Federal League. That challenge, begun in 1914, was yet another raid on the rosters and salary structures of the established leagues in an attempt to create a third "major" league. American League president Ban Johnson would have appreciated full well the tactics being employed as they were largely patterned after his successful attack on the National League at the start of the century. But Johnson's perspective was that of a baseball magnate, an owner. In the final negotiations over the fate of the Federals that produced what *Baseball Magazine* called at the time the Treaty of Cincinnati, it was Tener who stood up for the players and opposed the concerted effort by several owners to blacklist those who had jumped to the outlaw circuit. "If Organized Ball admits to fellowship and full membership the magnates who coaxed our players away from us," he said, "how can we consistently bar the players themselves?"[33]

As Tener's term as league president reached its midpoint in 1916, a writer for the same magazine offered this appraisal:

> In some quarters, there has been dissatisfaction that the president did not employ the "big stick" methods a little more, in other words, that he did not at once perform what was rendered impossible in the very nature of the league organization. But to those

who know affairs as they are [a reference to obstinate owners and the czar-like behavior of his American League counterpart, Ban Johnson], President Tener must appeal as the ablest executive the National League has ever had. . . ."[34]

After retiring from the game at the end of his term and returning to his banking career, Tener remained active in sports and was a frequent spectator at National League ballgames. He suffered a heart attack, his fourth, in May 1946 and died later that month, having outlived all nine of his siblings and even every member of his cabinet when he had been Governor.[35]

Finally, we come to the subsequent development of **the congressional baseball game** per se. We will take a longer view of this momentarily, but for now, let us limit ourselves to the immediate aftermath of the 1909 contest. With respect to the 1910 game, the short answer is that there wasn't one. Insofar as I have been able to ascertain, no one made any effort to organize a matchup between the parties in the second session of that Congress. If one accepts the notion that Tener was little more than a proximate agent of the GOP powers in advancing the first CBG, it is then worth noting that Speaker Cannon and his senior committee chairs had no reason to encourage such a game in the second session, as there was no pending legislation under consideration of the same magnitude as the tariff, and in any event, Cannon no longer could manipulate the workings of the House as he had the prior year. If, alternatively, one accepts the reports that Tener's organizing was in response to an initiative from John Garner to get some form of sporting revenge on the abusive majority in 1909, then consider, again, that the minority Democrats had no emotional impetus to do so because early in 1910 they had joined with the progressive Republicans in the House to strip Cannon of much of his power.

That brings us to the lingering possibility that it was, in fact, Tener himself who was the prime mover behind the game in 1909. In that instance, it is worth remembering that, though he was by mid-year 1910 the GOP candidate for governor of his home state, he was quite insistent upon holding onto his congressional seat until the very moment of his inauguration in 1911. And he was, by all accounts, a hail fellow well met, as the saying went—a man who greatly enjoyed his friendships upon and beyond the Hill. So, if he had conceived the game in 1909, and if such a good time had been had by all as seems to have been the case, why, as we asked just above, would he not seek to repeat the event the following year?

Whichever reason or explanation prevails, the net result was a net zero—no CBG2 in 1910.

But 1911 was different. It was in that year that the first real progress came toward institutionalizing the congressional baseball game. The record is silent on who took the lead in organizing the game, but Nick Longworth, who acted as captain of the GOP side, seems a likely choice. And the game seems to have generated a good deal of excitement on the Hill. One account likened the atmosphere in the House the morning of the game to children waiting for school to let out, with congressmen literally squirming in their seats waiting for dismissal.[36] Perhaps because of weather delays and the resulting scheduling conflicts, rather than American League Park, the match was played at Georgetown University. The lineups overlapped somewhat with those from two years earlier, but the prior experience does not appear to have improved the quality of play. The final score was closer—12-9, again in favor of the Democrats—but that may be because the players were so exhausted by the end of the fourth inning that they agreed to a motion to adjourn. As in 1909, the postgame coverage focused on the physical condition of the "athletes," including one article headlined, "Odor of Liniment Reigns Over House in Wake of Game."

An initial report had indicated that John Tener would return as one of the umpires, and another suggested that Victor Berger of Wisconsin, the House's lone Socialist Party representative and hence presumed to be a neutral observer, would fill such a role. But in the event, it was two partisans, future Supreme Court Justice, Secretary of State, and Governor James Byrnes of South Carolina for the Democrats and William Wilson of Illinois for the Republicans, who ruled the roost. The pair were frequently in disagreement, which they resolved by a series of coin flips. Byrnes flipped the coin each time and apparently won every flip. There is no record of whether Mr. Wilson ever asked to check the coin. There were two home runs in the game, one struck by Longworth that landed

Figure 24. The 1911 Republican team for CBG2. Front Row: Lafferty of Oregon, Kendall of Iowa, Longworth of Ohio, Porter of Pennsylvania, Slemp of Virginia. Back Row: Farr of Pennsylvania, Anderson of Minnesota, Reyburn of Pennsylvania, and Miller of Minnesota.

in the nearby C&O Canal and was stolen by a canal boat driver, and the other by Democrat Thomas Scully of New Jersey that landed in the car owned by Republican Ira Copley of Illinois, who was merely spectating.[37]

CBG2, played without political context or animosity, proved to be the true harbinger of games to come.

CBG: THE LEGACY

THE CONGRESSIONAL BASEBALL GAME. CBG. We know it today as an annual event on the charitable calendar in the Nation's Capital. After its irregular start as a strategic ploy to relieve political pressure in 1909 and its resurrection by Nick Longworth and others two years later, the game, which pits congressional Democrats against their Republican counterparts, has been played frequently through the intervening years and almost continuously since 1962 when it came under the sponsorship of *Roll Call*, a magazine focused on the political and policy activities of the Congress and read religiously by every Capitol Hill insider. Since 2016, the logistics of game and its community outreach have been overseen by a dedicated foundation, Congressional Sports for Charity, with the support of dozens of corporate and other sponsors.[1] At stake? Bragging rights for the year between the contests and a considerable sum of money that is divided among local charities in the capital city. Members of the Senate are not barred from participation, and over the years, a few have taken the field, but for reasons of relative age and infirmity, most who play in the game each year are members of the lower house. In 2024, as an example, more than 25,000 tickets to the game were sold at ten dollars apiece, and with added contributions, the game raised more than a million dollars for charity. Overall, the Republicans have won forty-six of the eighty-nine contests and the Democrats forty-two, with one nine-inning tie in 1983.

The 2024 contest, the latest at this writing, was broadcast nationally on the Fox Sports (FS1) Network and featured mid-game interviews with the leaders of both parties. But historically, news coverage of the games has been sporadic, mainly limited to the Washington, DC, market and other major markets in the east, along with those that are home to one or more of the "star" players. The coverage is almost invariably humorous. The participants may well take the competition seriously—and the many hours of practice and preparation they typically put in is solid evidence of that—but the sports and other journalists who cover the game clearly do not.

Since it first opened in 2008, Nationals Park has hosted the game, but the venue has hardly been fixed or consistent over the years. The first ten games (except CBG2) were played at American League Park, and the next sixteen at Griffith Stadium. The ten games that followed were played at D.C. Stadium or, as it was known from 1969 onward, Robert F. Kennedy (RFK) Stadium. There followed four games at Baltimore's Memorial Stadium, the nearest Major League ballpark once the Senators had abandoned Washington for the second time, then one game at Langley High School in McLean, VA, seventeen games at Four Mile Run Park in Alexandria, VA, and ten at Maryland's Prince George's County Stadium, before returning to RFK together with the new Washington Nationals franchise for three years until the new stadium could be completed.

There have been many gaps in that schedule. No game was played, for example, in 1910, which meant that the 1909 contest could well have been left as a one-off event. But the series resumed the following year, only to be suspended in 1920-1925, 1927, 1929-1931, 1934, 1936, 1940, 1942-1944, and 1958-1961. The occasional absence of the contest can be attributed to a variety of sources: the Great Depression, World War II, and even the intervention of a House Speaker, Sam Rayburn of Texas, who claimed the game was simply too physical. In 1914, Speaker Champ Clark did not halt the game, but when he found himself in need of a quorum, he dispatched the House Sergeant-at-Arms to the ballpark to bring the Members back to the chamber. It was only after *Roll Call* assumed the sponsorship that regularity was restored with the exception of the pandemic year of 2020. There was one other variant: in 1935, 1937-1939, and 1941, the game was played not between partisan opponents but between Members of Congress on one side and the reporters who covered them on the other.

The games themselves have been a mix of high- and low-scoring contests and of close and lopsided results. While the forty-two runs scored in 2024 matched the second-highest total for the series—that having been set in the very first matchup and exceeded only in a 22-21 nailbiter won by the Democrats in 1917—run totals in the twenties and thirties are not uncommon. And while that recent game was very one-sided, with the GOP winning 31-11, one- and two-run margins are also routine. As for that one tie game in 1983? The score after nine innings was knotted at 17-17—hardly a pitchers' duel. For those readers who are detail-oriented, Appendix 4 provides a table based on one maintained by the House of Representatives, showing the dates, locations, scores, and winning team of each game since the series began in 1909.[2]

To date, according to the official history, eleven so-called former professional baseball players have served in the House, including:

- John Thomas Hunt (umpired in the National League for three years in the 1890s),
- John Tener,
- William Oldfield (no supporting documentation found),
- Thomas McMillan (a shortstop and center fielder who played in four Major League seasons between 1908 and 1912, including time with the Brooklyn Superbas, Cincinnati Reds, and New York Yankees),
- Edward Austin Kelly (one year with the Boston Red Sox in 1914),
- Raymond Joseph Cannon (reportedly played semi-pro ball from 1908 to 1922),
- James Prioleau Richards (played baseball at the University of South Carolina but turned down a proffered major league contract when he graduated),
- Pius Louis Schwert (two years with the Yankees, 1914-1915),
- Cecil William "Runt" Bishop (played second base in the Kitty [for Kentucky-Illinois-Tennessee] League and declined an offer to play in the Yankees farm system),

- Wilmer David "Vinegar Bend" Mizell (nine years between 1952 and 1962 with the St. Louis Cardinals, Pittsburgh Pirates, and New York Mets) and
- James Paul David Bunning (whose seventeen-year career in the majors, 1955-1971, included time with the Detroit Tigers, Philadelphia Phillies, Pittsburgh Pirates, and Los Angeles Dodgers, not to mention a perfect game he pitched on Father's Day 1964).[3]

This history excludes a twelfth player, Roger Williams, who was drafted by the Atlanta Braves out of college and played in the team's minor league system for several years. Several of these former players have participated in the annual CBG over the years, and at least two, Bishop and Williams, have managed one of the squads for several years.

The first home run in a congressional baseball game occurred in the very first game—a three-run "shot" by Democrat Joseph O'Connell of Massachusetts, and the first grand slam was hit in 1957 by a future President of the United States, Gerald R. Ford. The record for most runs scored in a single inning belongs to the Democrats of 1928, who plated twenty runners in the second inning on their way to a 36-4 rout of the GOP. The first radio broadcast of the game came in that same year on WRC radio in Washington.[4] Ronald Dellums of California and Delegate Walter Fauntroy of the District of Columbia broke the color barrier in 1971, while Ileana Ros-Lehtinen of Florida, Maria Cantwell of Washington state, and Blanche Lincoln Lamber of Arkansas were the first women to play, all in 1993. In 1963, neither team could provide a pitcher, so George Susce, a reliever for the Senators, took the mound for both.

The game has had its heroes. In 2005, for example, Republican pitcher John Shimkus of Illinois was still recovering from open-heart surgery and was not supposed to take the mound in the game. But when the GOP starter, Senator John Ensign of Nevada, was called back to the Capitol for an important evening vote, Shimkus came on to close out the sixth inning before Ensign could return for the remainder of the game. "It probably wasn't the smartest thing I've ever done," he is reported to have said afterward.[5]

Over the years, the game has not been without political controversy, though unlike 1909, that typically comes from external more than internal sources. The 2024 game, for example, was interrupted for about fifteen minutes during the second inning of play while police chased and tackled a small number of climate activists who had chosen to disrupt the event. More serious was an incident in 2017, not during the game but in a pregame practice session, when a 66-year-old gunman from Illinois opened fire on the GOP team, badly wounding Congressman and then-GOP Whip Steve Scalise of Louisiana and four others, including two Capitol policemen, before being shot to death himself. Scalise survived the attack owing to the rapid action of a colleague and former Iraq War combat surgeon, Brad Wenstrup of Ohio, now a podiatrist, who cut his pants leg and took steps to stop the bleeding.[6]

The occasional competitive disagreement notwithstanding—and these date to the very first game when the parties had difficulty agreeing on the umpiring crew—one clear theme emerges in virtually all the news coverage of congressional games through the years: A good time was had by all. Baseball has always served as a unifying force, one capable of overcoming even the most fundamental partisan and political disagreements and bridging the differences between the most ardent partisans through their shared love of the game. Whether it is a Democrat like Mike Doyle of Pennsylvania ("When people say, 'Why can't you guys just get along,' I always tell them about the friendships I make in baseball. I had a chance to develop relationships with Republicans that I wouldn't have had if I didn't play baseball.") or a Republican like Kevin Brady of Texas ("I think it's one of the most important bipartisan events we still have on Capitol Hill. We really like each other. I think it creates just great camaraderie and relationships with members of the other team.") the references to enhanced comity arising from the game are abundant. Perhaps the aforementioned Congressman Shimkus captured it best when he said, "All I know is that I love to play the game of baseball, I love to practice, and I love the camaraderie."[7]

All of this we know. And we know as well the delivered origin story of the very first CBG in 1909. It was all the doing of one of those former professional players, John Tener. He thought of it, he organized it, he played in it. But that story is wanting in detail, context, and accuracy.

This is, after all, the *congressional* baseball game we are talking about. And while it may be the conventional wisdom that CBG1 was some sort of casual or pick-up game initiated by Tener, the reality appears to have been rather more political and a good deal more intriguing. Baseball—long accepted as the national pastime but newly proclaimed just two years earlier, in 1907, in the Doubleday myth, promulgated by none other than Tener's former boss, Albert Spalding, as "the" truly American sport—may have been the political equivalent of a prescription medication, one expected to cure the symptoms of a range of uniquely congressional aches and pains. In the end, as we have seen, it seems instead to have caused some literal aches and pains, while the curative powers of the game were, at best, short-lived.

THE LAST ACT (LITERALLY)

NINETEEN-NINE WAS AN event-filled year in American history. American troops were withdrawn from Cuba, where they had been stationed since the Spanish-American War in 1898, and Teddy Roosevelt's Great White Fleet came home after circling the globe. Roosevelt himself left for a year on safari in Africa, allowing some breathing space for his newly-elected successor, William Howard Taft. The U.S. Army purchased its first military airplane, choosing the Wright Flyer over its Curtiss competitor. The Navy established a base at Pearl Harbor, Hawaii, and Robert Peary claimed to have reached the North Pole. Barry Goldwater, Dean Rusk, Clyde Barrow, Eudora Welty, Edwin Land, and Leo Fender, among countless others, entered the world. And the Payne-Aldrich Tariff Act became law.

In baseball that year, the first steel and concrete stadiums were built in Philadelphia (Shibe Park) and Pittsburgh (Forbes Field)—the game's answer to the tendency of wooden grandstands to catch fire. Washington would, as we have seen, follow suit two years later. Ty Cobb led the Major Leagues in home runs with nine; his Tigers met the Pirates in a World Series that pitted the rising Tigers star against Honus Wagner, the Pittsburgh veteran. Wagner bested Cobb, and the Pirates bested Detroit. The American Tobacco Company released the first two sets of baseball cards that would later be known as the T206 cards, the most prized cards among present-day collectors, as free premiums in boxes of cigarettes. Cleveland Naps shortstop Neal Ball completed the first unassisted triple play of the modern era. Philadelphia Athletics catcher Doc

Powers slammed into the new concrete wall while chasing a foul ball in the inaugural game at Shibe Park; he died two weeks later of his injuries. Harry Pulliam, president of the National League, shot himself in the head and died. And in Washington, the first congressional baseball game was played, with the Democrats defeating the Republicans 26-16.

But fittingly, the final act of our tale takes us back to the halls of Congress. On August 5, 1909, after waiting around in a small room in the Capitol for an hour while Congress made some last-minute corrections to the legislation, President Taft signed the Payne-Aldrich Tariff Act. But over in the House chamber, as business wound down for the session, and very shortly after Speaker Cannon had at last named the committees and their members, there was one final piece of legislation introduced. The very last bill of the session, known as H.R. 12260, was introduced by Representative Harry M. Coudrey, Republican of Missouri. At the time, Coudrey was embroiled in a small scandal involving the sale to members of Congress of discounted shares of stock in the Mississippi Transportation Company, which planned to build barges to carry goods on the Mississippi River and was seeking congressional appropriations to build a channel for their vessels from Chicago to the Gulf of Mexico. The matter was revealed to the public by Paul Howland of Ohio, best known here as the first baseman for the GOP in CBG1, who proclaimed that he could not make so unethical a purchase. Asked then about the twenty-five congressmen who had purchased the shares, Coudrey responded, "We did not sell them this stock to influence their vote on the appropriation which will be asked for, but to give the company prestige by having these congressmen identified with it."[1] Two years later, in November 1911, Coudrey would be indicted separately in New York State for engaging in a fraudulent insurance scheme.[2]

But on August 5, 1909, just three days before the stock scandal was made public, Mr. Coudrey's attentions were directed elsewhere. H.R. 12260 called for imposing a tax of $50 per week or $10 per day on all baseball parks in the District of Columbia where baseball games were played and to which admission was charged.[3] It was the closing act of the House of Representatives in the Special Session of the Sixty-First Congress. And it seems a fitting one. From the machinations on the tariff to Oriole Park in Baltimore to the aesthetic ugliness of the first congressional baseball game to the pages of the *Congressional Record*, one point seems to hold true. With apologies to Benjamin Franklin, if not to Charley Dryden, it is this:

> In this world, nothing can be said to be certain
> except baseball and taxes.

CHOOSING SIDES

Baseball, they say, has changed a heap; I guess it has, in spots,
And yet I liked it better when we played it on the lots.
There were no signs for 'hit and run,' no dazzling 'fadeaways,'
We had no high-priced managers to tell us fancy plays.
No, we were just a lot of kids, with tanned and freckled hides;
There were no concrete grandstands when we played at 'choosing sides.'

I saw a ball game yesterday, and o'er a brass band's flare.
The cheers of thirty thousand fans were soaring in the air,
The turnstiles had been clicking for three solid golden hours,
Recording wealth and profit for the big-league base ball powers.
How soon we lose our play days! How swiftly childhood glides!
There were no clicking turnstiles when we played at 'choosing sides.'

The captains used to toss a bat, and then, hand over hand –
But why repeat a story every boy must understand?
Then came the careful picking—'I'll take Reddy.' 'Give me Flynn.'
'I'll choose you, Skinny Murphy.' 'I'll take you, Pat McGinn.'
They picked the live one first, of course, and finished with the snides.
Feelings were often ruffled when we played at 'choosing sides.'

Dear reader, you'll remember, if you peek into the past,
The little four-eyed fellow that was always chosen last,
The little weak-kneed urchin that the captain would ignore
Until he found, by counting, that he needed one man more.
He couldn't bat, he couldn't field, and yet that shrimp today
Is making laws in congress while his captain drives a dray.

William T. Kirk, 1911[1]

APPENDIX 1: THE PLAYERS[1]
THE DEMOCRATS

1. Finis Garrett, Tennessee 9, 2B

F. J. GARRETT, Tennessee
Second Base
DEMOCRATS

AB	R	H	PO	A	E
3	3	3	1	0	1

Born in 1875 in Ore Springs, Tennessee, Garrett was 34 years old when he took the field. He served in the House from 1905-1929, and between 1923 and 1929 served as Chair of the Democratic Caucus and Minority Leader. In 1929, he was appointed by Calvin Coolidge to the Court of Customs and Patent Appeals, and in 1937, he was promoted by Franklin Roosevelt to be the Presiding (Chief) Judge of that court, serving in that position until 1955. Garrett received an A.B. from Bethel College in 1897, read law in 1899, and worked as a newspaper editor and teacher before entering politics. He died in 1956 at the age of 80.

1a.* J. Thomas Heflin, Alabama 5, LF

J. T. HEFLIN, Alabama
Left Field
DEMOCRATS

AB	R	H	PO	A	E
1	0	1	0	0	2

"Cotton Tom" Heflin was born in Louina, Alabama, in 1869 and was 41 years old on game day. He attended Alabama A&M (now Auburn University) and, after reading law, was admitted to the bar in 1893. Heflin served in the House from 1904-1920 and in the Senate from 1920-1931. He was a staunch segregationist, and in 1908, was involved in an incident in which he threw a black rider who had confronted him off a Washington streetcar and fired a pistol at him. The charges against him were dismissed. It was Heflin in 1914 who introduced the legislation creating Mother's Day. He died in 1951 at age 82.

* Entered the game as a substitute when O'Connell moved to 2B, replacing Garrett.

2. William Hughes, New Jersey 6, 1B

W. HUGHES, New Jersey
First Base
DEMOCRATS

AB	R	H	PO	A	E
6	3	2	8	1	1

Born in 1872 in County Louth, Ireland, Hughes served in the House from 1903-1905 and 1907-1912, then in the Senate from 1913-1918. He was a stenographer and labor activist, then, after service in the Spanish-American War, studied the law and became a labor lawyer. In Congress, he was a voice for the agenda of the American Federation of Labor and, in 1913, played a central role in crafting the Underwood Tariff Act that reduced the Payne-Aldrich tariffs. He died in 1918 at the age of 46.

3. James McDermott, Illinois 4, 2B, CF

J. T. MCDERMOTT, Illinois
Second Base - Center Field
DEMOCRATS

AB	R	H	PO	A	E
6	4	3	3	4	0

Born in 1872 in Grand Rapids, Michigan, McDermott was 37 years old in July 1909. He taught telegraphy for five years in Detroit, then moved to Chicago, where he was a tobacconist, and then served in the House from 1907-1917. Upon leaving Congress, McDermott returned to Chicago and his retail business. He died there of heart disease in 1938 at the age of 65.

4. William Oldfield, Arkansas 2, C, CF

W. A. OLDFIELD, Arkansas
Catcher - Center Field
DEMOCRATS

AB	R	H	PO	A	E
6	2	3	3	1	0

Oldfield was born in Franklin, Arkansas, in 1874. He entered the House in 1909 and served through 1928, serving as Chair of the Committee on Patents and later as Minority Whip. Oldfield graduated from Arkansas College in 1896 and worked as a teacher and school principal. Following service in the Spanish-American War, he studied law at Cumberland University and became a county prosecutor. After a failed run in 1906, he began his congressional career in the next cycle and was reelected in 1928, but died in November of that year at the age of 52.

5. Eugene Kinkead, New Jersey 9, LF, C, Captain

E. F. KINKEAD, New Jersey
Left Field - Catcher
DEMOCRATS

AB	R	H	PO	A	E
6	3	3	3	0	0

Born in 1876 to American parents in County Cork, Ireland, Kinkead was a freshman in the House when he captained the team in CBG1. A graduate of Seton Hall College in 1895, he was president of the Jersey Railway Advertising Company and Orange Publishing, and in 1898, was president of the Jersey City Board of Aldermen. Kinkead served in the House from 1909-1915, then briefly as a county sheriff. He was a major in military intelligence in World War I and later an executive of Colonial Trust Company in New York. He died in 1960.

6. Joe T. Robinson, Arkansas 6, RF

J. T. ROBINSON, Arkansas
Right Field
DEMOCRATS

AB	R	H	PO	A	E
3	3	3	1	0	1

Born in 1872 in Lonoke County, Arkansas, Robinson was 37 years old in 1909 and in his fourth term in Congress. Robinson received an LLB from the University of Virginia. He served in the House from 1903-1913. He was elected Governor of Arkansas in 1912 but resigned after two months to take a seat in the Senate, where he served from 1913 until he died in 1937. Robinson was the last Senator elected by a state legislature rather than by direct popular vote. A progressive leader, he served as Chair of the Senate Democratic Caucus and as both Minority and Majority Leader, in the latter of which positions he was responsible for passing New Deal legislation. Robinson was Al Smith's running mate in the unsuccessful presidential campaign of 1928.

7. Daniel Driscoll, New York 35, SS, 3B

D. A. DRISCOLL, New York
Shortstop - Third Base
DEMOCRATS

AB	R	H	PO	A	E
4	1	0	2	1	0

Driscoll was born in Buffalo, New York, in 1875. After completing high school, he joined his father's undertaking business before entering politics. He served in the House from 1909-1917, and when he lost a bid for reelection in 1916 resumed his earlier work as an undertaker. He was postmaster of Buffalo from 1934-1937 and also president of the local Phoenix Brewing Company. Driscoll died in 1955 at the age of 80.

8. Joseph Francis O'Connell, Massachusetts 10, 3b, SS

J. F. O'CONNELL, Mass.
Third Base - Shortstop
DEMOCRATS

AB	R	H	PO	A	E
3	3	3	1	0	1

O'Connell was born in Boston in 1872 and graduated from Boston College, where he helped form the school's first football team, in 1893 and from the law department at Harvard University in 1896. His legal career was briefly interrupted by his service in the House from 1907-1911. From 1914 until he died in 1942, he served by continual reappointment on the National Conference on Uniform State Laws, making him one of the nation's most influential voices on state-level legislation. He was a professor of law at Suffolk Law School and served as vice president of the school's board of trustees. O'Connell ran unsuccessfully for the Senate in 1930 and for Mayor of Boston in 1933. He died in Boston at age 70 in 1942.

9. Edwin Webb, North Carolina 9, P

E. Y. WEBB, North Carolina
Pitcher
DEMOCRATS

AB	R	H	PO	A	E
5	3	3	0	2	0

Born in 1872 in Shelby, North Carolina, Webb was 37 years old at the time of CBG1. He was a graduate of Wake Forest College and studied law at the University of North Carolina, Chapel Hill, joining the bar in 1894. He extended his legal education at the University of Virginia. He was a trustee of both Wake Forest and the A&M College of Raleigh (now North Carolina State University). Webb served in the House from 1903-1919, where he chaired the Committee on the Judiciary for six years. In 1919 he was appointed by Woodrow Wilson as a judge of the U.S District Court for the western district of North Carolina. Webb retired from the judiciary in 1948 and passed away in 1955.

THE REPUBLICANS

1. W. Aubrey Thomas, Ohio 19, 3B

W. A. THOMAS, Ohio
Third Base
REPUBLICANS

AB	R	H	PO	A	E
5	1	2	0	0	1

Born in 1866 in Y Bynea, Wales, Thomas was among the oldest players in CBG1 at age 43. He attended Mount Union College and Rensselaer Polytechnic Institute and worked as an analytical chemist in the iron and steel industry. A member of both the Masons and the Elks, he was president of the Mahoning Valley Steel Company and a director of Niles Firebrick. Thomas served in the House from 1904 to 1911 but lost a reelection bid in 1910. He moved to Alabama in 1918, where he was president of the Jenifer Iron Company. Thomas died in 1951 at age 85.

2. Ralph Cole, Ohio 8, RF

R. D. COLE, Ohio
Right Field
REPUBLICANS

AB	R	H	PO	A	E
6	3	4	0	0	1

Ralph Cole was born in Vanlue, Ohio, in 1873 and graduated from Findlay College in 1896. He studied law at Ohio Northern University while working as a deputy county clerk and was admitted to the bar in 1900. After four years in the state legislature, he was elected to the House, where he served from 1905-1911. He was not renominated in 1910, another victim of the anti-Cannon purge. He served as a legal advisor to the Comptroller of the Currency, then enlisted in the U.S. Army in 1917, serving overseas and rising to the rank of lieutenant colonel in the Infantry. In 1919, he was one of the founders of the American Legion. After the war, he resumed his legal practice. Cole died in 1932 of injuries sustained in a traffic accident.

3. Albert Foster Dawson, Iowa 2, 2B

A. F. DAWSON, Iowa
Second Base
REPUBLICANS

AB	R	H	PO	A	E
4	4	3	2	0	0

Born in 1872 in Spragueville, Iowa, Dawson was educated at the University of Wisconsin-Madison and, in 1891, entered the newspaper business, including three years as city editor of the *Clinton* Herald. While a staffer on Capitol Hill, he studied finance at Columbian University (now The George Washington University). He served in the House from 1905 to 1911 but declined to run in 1910. He also declined an offer to serve as private secretary to President Taft. Returning to Iowa, from 1911 until 1929, he served as president of the First National Bank of Davenport, then worked in the public utility industry until 1945. Dawson passed away on a train in 1949.

4. John Tener, Pennsylvania 24, SS, Captain

J. K. TENER, Pennsylvania
Shortstop
REPUBLICANS

AB	R	H	PO	A	E
6	3	2	3	7	1

Tener's biography has already been presented in detail. The basics: He was born in 1863 in County Tyrone in what is now Northern Ireland, making him the oldest player in CBG1. He pitched in the National League for two years and the Players League for one and was an important participant in the 1889 Spalding World Tour. After that, Tener was a banker and industrialist, a member of the House for a single term (1909-1911), Governor of Pennsylvania, and President of the National League. In 1926 he sought the gubernatorial nomination for a second time but was passed over. In the 1930s, Tener served as a director of the Philadelphia Phillies. He died in Pittsburgh in 1946.

5. L. Paul Howland, Ohio 20, 1B

L. P. HOWLAND, Ohio
First Base
REPUBLICANS

AB	R	H	PO	A	E
5	2	3	7	0	2

Born in Jefferson, Ohio, in 1865, Howland graduated from Oberlin College in 1887 and from the law department of Harvard University in 1890. He practiced law mainly in Cleveland and served as a volunteer in the Spanish-American War. Howland served three terms in the House (1907-1913), surviving the Democratic advances of 1910 but losing a reelection bid in 1912. He resumed his law practice at that point. Howland died in Cleveland in 1942 at age 77.

6. Butler Ames, Massachusetts 5, LF

B. AMES, Massachusetts
Left Field
REPUBLICANS

AB	R	H	PO	A	E
5	1	3	0	0	0

Son of Adelbert Ames and grandson of Benjamin Franklin Butler, both decorated Union generals during the Civil War, Ames was born in 1871 in Lowell, Massachusetts. He was 38 years old on game day. Ames attended Phillips Exeter Academy and graduated from West Point in 1894. Rather than pursue a military career, he next attended MIT, where he graduated in 1896 as a mechanical and electrical engineer. He rejoined the Army during the Spanish-American War, rising to the rank of lieutenant colonel. After a single term in the state legislature, Ames served in the House from 1903-1913. Foregoing reelection, he then held a variety of corporate executive positions. He died in 1954 at age 83.

7. Nicholas Longworth, Ohio 1, CF

N. LONGWORTH, Ohio
Center Field
REPUBLICANS

AB	R	H	PO	A	E
4	1	4	0	0	1

Longworth was born in 1869 into a prominent and powerful family in Cincinnati, Ohio. He graduated from Harvard University in 1891, then studied law at Harvard and the Cincinnati Law School, graduating in 1894. He entered politics at the local level in 1898, worked his way up through the Ohio House and Senate, and was elected to Congress in 1903, serving almost continuously until 1931. In 1906, he married Alice Roosevelt, the president's daughter, in a White House ceremony. Longworth sided with the Cannon conservatives in 1909 and after. When he rose to Speaker in 1925, he worked to restore many of the powers that had been taken away from Cannon and also expelled a group of progressives from the GOP Caucus. Longworth died of pneumonia while visiting South Carolina in 1931.

8. James Francis Burke, Pennsylvania 31, C

J. F. BURKE, Pennsylvania
Catcher
REPUBLICANS

AB	R	H	PO	A	E
4	1	4	10	0	2

Burke was born in Petroleum Center, Pennsylvania, in 1867 and graduated from the University of Michigan in 1892. While at Michigan, he
organized a predecessor group that later became the College Republicans.
Burke practiced law in Pennsylvania and was secretary of the Republican
National Committee in 1892 but resigned to work full-time as president
of the group he had founded. He served in the House from 1905-1915
and chaired the congressional committee that inaugurated President
Taft in 1909. Burke chaired the Committee on Education and played
an active role in drafting the Federal Reserve Act. He served as Director
of War Savings during World War I. He was an avid sportsman and was
tasked by the U.S. Golf Association with drafting a set of rules for the
game. Burke died in 1932.

9. Joseph Gaines, West Virginia 3, P

J. H. GAINES, West Virginia
Pitcher
REPUBLICANS

AB	R	H	PO	A	E
4	0	1	0	1	1

Born in Washington, DC, in 1864, at 45 years of age Gaines was the second oldest player in CBG1 after John Tener. After his family moved to West Virginia, he attended West Virginia University and then graduated from Princeton College in 1886. Admitted to the bar in 1887, he was named as U.S. Attorney for West Virginia by President McKinley in 1897. Gaines served in Congress from 1901-1911 and chaired the Committee on Election(s). Gaines failed of reelection in 1910 and returned to the practice of law. He died in 1951.

NP. **Edward Vreeland, New York 37, Injured Reserve**

E. B. VREELAND, New York
Injured
REPUBLICANS

AB	R	H	PO	A	E
0	0	0	0	0	0

Born in 1856 in Cuba, New York, had he not injured himself so seriously while practicing, at 53, Vreeland would have been by nearly a decade the senior member on the field for CBG1. Vreeland served as superintendent of the Salamanca, NY, public schools from 1877-1882, then held positions in the banking, oil, and insurance businesses before becoming president of the Salamanca Trust Company in 1892. He served in Congress from 1899-1913 and was Chairman of the Committee on Banking and Currency. He was vice chairman of the National Monetary Commission from 1909-1912. After retiring from Congress, he returned to his business pursuits in Salamanca, where he died in 1936.

APPENDIX 2: THE TARIFF REFORM CALENDAR[1]

SIXTY-FIRST CONGRESS, SPECIAL SESSION
1909

15-Mar	President Taft convenes a special session
16-Mar	Adoption of rules for the session
	Taft states purpose of the session as tariff revision
	Speaker Joe Cannon declines to name standing committees
17-Mar	Sereno Payne introduces H.R. 1438, pre-drafted reform bill
	Bill referred to Ways & Means Committee
18-Mar	Ways & Means reports bill back to House
19-Mar	Debate on bill begins with limited amendments allowed
9-Apr	House passes Payne bill 217-161, refers to Senate
	On Nelson Aldrich motion, bill sent to Finance Committee
12-Apr	Finance Committee reports bill back to Senate
19-Apr	Senate opens floor debate
16-Jun	Taft calls for income tax amendment
22-Jun	John Tener arranges group visit to Orioles game
23-Jun	Tener, Payne, others attend Orioles game, talk tariffs
28-Jun	Aldrich introduces S.J.R. 40, income tax amendment, in Senate
	House considers amendment as joint resolution
8-Jul	Senate passes bill with 847 amendments including a new corporate income tax 45-34, 13 not voting
9-Jul	House non-concurs with (rejects) Senate version of bill
9-Jul	House and Senate agree to hold a conference on the bill
12-Jul	Sixteenth Amendment passes both houses, sent to states for ratification
15-Jul	Taft proposes his own amendments
16-Jul	Playing of First Congressional Baseball Game
30-Jul	Conference report presented to House
31-Jul	House passes conference report 195-183, 10 not voting

5-Aug	Senate passes conference report 70-22
	President signs Payne-Aldrich Tariff Act
	Speaker Cannon finally appoints all standing committees
	Congress adjourns

APPENDIX 3:
TIMELINE OF BASEBALL TEAMS AND PLAYING FIELDS IN WASHINGTON, 1859–1909

YEAR	TEAM/LEAGUE	ACTION
1859	Washington Nationals Baseball Club formed	
1867	Nationals build winner, conduct western exhibition tour	16th & S Streets, White House Lot
1869	First recorded Nationals game played	White (House) Lot
1876	National League establishes claim as the first "major" league	
1884	Nationals join American Association; team folds	Athletic Park
	Nationals join Union Association mid-season	Capitol Grounds (AKA, Union Association Grounds)
1885	Union Association disbands	
1886	Nationals join National League	Capital Park Grounds (AKA, Swampoodle Grounds)
1889	Nationals dropped from the National League	
1891	Washington Nationals/Statesmen join American Association	Boundary Field
1892	American Association folds	
	Nationals rejoin National League	Boundary Field (AKA, National Park)
1900	Nationals dropped from the National League	
1901	Western Association rebrands as the American League	
	Nationals/Senators join American League	American League Park (I)

YEAR	TEAM/LEAGUE	ACTION
1904		American League Park (II) (AKA, National Park)
1909	First Congressional Baseball Game played	American League Park

APPENDIX 4: HISTORY OF THE CONGRESSIONAL BASEBALL GAME[1]

Year	Location	Winner	Score
1909	American League Park	Democrats	26-16
1911	Georgetown University	Democrats	12-9
1912	National Park (same as American League Park)	Democrats	21-20
1913	National Park	Democrats	29-4
1914	National Park	Democrats	16-9
1915	National Park	Democrats	
1916	National Park	Republicans	18-13
1917	National Park	Democrats	22-21
1918	National Park	Republicans	19-5
1919	National Park	Republicans	
1926	Griffith Stadium	Democrats	12-9
1928	Griffith Stadium	Democrats	36-4
1932	Griffith Stadium	Republicans	19-5
1933	Griffith Stadium	Republicans	18-16
1945	Griffith Stadium	Democrats	
1946	Griffith Stadium	Democrats	
1947	Griffith Stadium	Republicans	16-13
1948	Griffith Stadium	Democrats	23-14
1949	Griffith Stadium	Democrats	16-10
1950	Griffith Stadium	Democrats	8-4
1951	Griffith Stadium	Democrats	7-3
1952	Griffith Stadium	Democrats	6-3
1953	Griffith Stadium	Democrats	3-2
1954	Griffith Stadium	Democrats	2-1
1955	Griffith Stadium	Republicans	12-4
1956	Griffith Stadium	Republicans	8-7

Year	Location	Winner	Score
1957	Griffith Stadium	Democrats	10-9
1962	D.C. Stadium	Republicans	4-0
1963	D.C. Stadium	Democrats	11-0
1964	D.C. Stadium	Republicans	6-5
1965	D.C. Stadium	Republicans	3-1
1966	D.C. Stadium	Republicans	14-7
1967	D.C. Stadium	Republicans	9-7
1968	D.C. Stadium	Republicans	16-1
1969	D.C. Stadium	Republicans	6-2
1970	D.C. Stadium	Republicans	6-4
1971	D.C. Stadium	Republicans	7-3
1972	D.C. Stadium	Republicans	7-2
1973	Memorial Stadium (Baltimore)	Republicans	12-4
1974	Memorial Stadium (Baltimore)	Republicans	7-3
1975	Memorial Stadium (Baltimore)	Democrats	3-2
1976	Memorial Stadium (Baltimore)	Democrats	5-4
1977	Langley HS (McLean, VA)	Republicans	7-6
1978	Four Mile Run Park (Arlington, VA)	Republicans	4-3
1979	Four Mile Run Park (Arlington, VA)	Democrats	7-3
1980	Four Mile Run Park (Arlington, VA)	Democrats	21-9
1981	Four Mile Run Park (Arlington, VA)	Republicans	6-4
1982	Four Mile Run Park (Arlington, VA)	Democrats	7-5
1983	Four Mile Run Park (Arlington, VA)	Tie	17-17
1984	Four Mile Run Park (Arlington, VA)	Republicans	13-4
1985	Four Mile Run Park (Arlington, VA)	Republicans	9-3
1986	Four Mile Run Park (Arlington, VA)	Democrats	8-6
1987	Four Mile Run Park (Arlington, VA)	Democrats	15-14
1988	Four Mile Run Park (Arlington, VA)	Republicans	14-13
1989	Four Mile Run Park (Arlington, VA)	Republicans	8-2
1990	Four Mile Run Park (Arlington, VA)	Republicans	9-6
1991	Four Mile Run Park (Arlington, VA)	Democrats	13-9
1992	Four Mile Run Park (Arlington, VA)	Republicans	11-7
1993	Four Mile Run Park (Arlington, VA)	Democrats	13-1

Year	Location	Winner	Score
1994	Four Mile Run Park (Arlington, VA)	Democrats	9-2
1995	Prince George's Stadium (Bowie, MD)	Republicans	6-0
1996	Prince George's Stadium (Bowie, MD)	Democrats	16-4
1997	Prince George's Stadium (Bowie, MD)	Republicans	10-9
1998	Prince George's Stadium (Bowie, MD)	Republicans	4-1
1999	Prince George's Stadium (Bowie, MD)	Republicans	17-1
2000	Prince George's Stadium (Bowie, MD)	Democrats	13-8
2001	Prince George's Stadium (Bowie, MD)	Republicans	9-1
2002	Prince George's Stadium (Bowie, MD)	Republicans	9-2
2003	Prince George's Stadium (Bowie, MD)	Republicans	5-3
2004	Prince George's Stadium (Bowie, MD)	Republicans	14-7
2005	RFK Stadium (DC)	Republicans	19-10
2006	RFK Stadium (DC)	Republicans	12-1
2007	RFK Stadium (DC)	Republicans	5-2
2008	Nationals Park	Republicans	11-10
2009	Nationals Park	Democrats	15-10
2010	Nationals Park	Democrats	13-5
2011	Nationals Park	Democrats	8-2
2012	Nationals Park	Democrats	18-5
2013	Nationals Park	Democrats	22-0
2014	Nationals Park	Democrats	15-6
2015	Nationals Park	Democrats	5-2
2016	Nationals Park	Republicans	8-7
2017	Nationals Park	Democrats	11-2
2018	Nationals Park	Democrats	21-5
2019	Nationals Park	Democrats	14-7
2021	Nationals Park	Republicans	13-12
2022	Nationals Park	Republicans	10-0
2023	Nationals Park	Republicans	16-6
2024	Nationals Park	Republicans	31-11

NOTES: As of 2024, the Democrats have won 42 of these games, the Republicans 46, and there has been one recorded tie. In 1935, 1937, 1938, 1939 and 1941, games were played between a bipartisan group of congressmen on one side and members of the press on the other. The 2020 game was canceled because of the COVID-19 pandemic.

ENDNOTES

1. Cited in Susan Ratcliffe, *Oxford Essential Quotations* (Fifth Ed.). New York: Oxford University Press, 2017, and accessed December 14, 2024, at https://www.oxfordreference.com/display/10.1093/acref/9780191843730.001.0001/q-oro-ed5-00002969.
2. "Casey Stengel Quotes," *Baseball Almanac*, accessed December 14, 2024, at https://www.baseball-almanac.com/quotes/quosteng.shtml.
3. Allen Sangree, "Lure of the Diamond," *Sunday Magazine of The (Washington) Sunday Star*, June 30, 1907, p. 17.

This Field, This Game

1. Tim Hagerty has done a nice job of cataloguing hundreds of these at the minor league level. See *Tales from the Dugout: 1,001 Humorous, Inspirational & Wild Anecdotes from Minor League Baseball*. Nashville, TN: Cider Mill Press, 2023.
2. "Speedway Produces Fine Balloon Crop," *The Indianapolis News*, June 5, 1909, p. 12; "Balloon Rope Spoils Catch," Associated Press as published in *The South Bend Tribune*, June 22, 1909, p. 2; and "A Lynching Narrowly Avoided," *Rochester Democrat & Chronicle*, June 24, 1909, p. 6.
3. "Eight Players Participate in Double Play: Ball Thrown 18 Times Before Runners Are Out," *The Washington Post*, August 15, 1909, p. 3.

Three Guys Walked into a Bar

1. "Ned Hanlon As Host: He Will Entertain a Congressional Party at Oriole Park," *Baltimore Sun*, June 23, 1909, p. 10; and "Noted Men to See Game: Representatives From Several States to Be Guests of President Hanlon," *Washington Evening Star*, June 23, 1909, p. 14.
2. See "Crumpacker Wants to Use Axe on Tariff," *Muncie* (Indiana) *Morning Star*, January 16, 1909, p. 1; and "Convention for Tariff Reforms in Great Start," *Richmond* (Indiana) *Evening Item*, February 16, 1909, pp. 1, 5.
3. "Day of Oratory in Choice of Senator," *The Indianapolis News*, January 19, 1909, pp. 1, 3.
4. With regard to Fisher, see "In the Mid-Continent Oil Fields," *Independence* (Kansas) *Daily Reporter*, May 18, 1909, p. 3; and Untitled, *Coffeeville* (Kansas) *Daily Bee*, May 17, 1909, p. 2.
5. "Resolution of Thanks: For Congressmen Who Made a Fight for the Tax Repeal," *Mayfield* (Kentucky) *Messenger*, April 26, 1909, p. 3. See also "Hon. J.W. Byrns Writes Letter to President Chas. H. Fort," *The Leaf Chronicle* (Clarksville, Tennessee), July 20, 1909, p. 5.
6. "Ned Hanlon As Host," op. cit.
7. "Ready for Business," Baltimore *Sun*, June 23, 1909, p. 11.
8. "Washington News," *The National Tribune* (Washington, D.C.), July 1, 1909, p. 5.
9. See "US Route 1 in Maryland," found online November 20, 2023, at https://en.wikipedia.org/wiki/U.S._Route_1_in_Maryland; and *Small Structures on Maryland's Roadways, Historic Context Report* (Baltimore: Maryland State Highway Administration, June 1997), Chapter 2, accessed June 29, 2024, at https://roads.maryland.gov/OPPEN/Small%20Structures%20on%20Maryland%27s%20Roadways,%20Historic%20Context%20Report.pdf#page=81&%23zoom=100.
10. Accounts of the trip and game are based primarily on "Stanley Is the Goods: Pitches Orioles to Victory, While Congressmen Watch," *Baltimore Sun*, June 24, 1909, p. 9; and "Guests of Hanlon: Statesmen Saw Orioles Beat Montreal," *The Sporting News*, July 1, 1909. Additional, and sometimes more accurate, details are drawn from "Noted Men to See Game: Representatives From Several States to Be Guests of President Hanlon," *Washington Evening Star*, June 23, 1909, p. 14; "Congressmen See Game," *The Washington Post*, June 24, 1909, p. 9; and Ray Hill, "Mr. Speaker: J.W. Byrns of Tennessee" (undated), reproduced in *The Knoxville Sentinel*, January 21, 2024, accessed at https://www.knoxfocus.com/archives/this-weeks-focus/mr-speaker-joseph-w-byrns-tennessee/.

11. "Congressmen on Tariff: Visitors to Baseball Game Talk of 'Revision Downward,'" *Baltimore Sun*, June 24, 1909, p. 12.

12. Jason Best, "A.G. Mills," accessed January 4, 2025, at https://sabr.org/bioproj/person/a-g-mills/.

13. "Girl Fears Not to Stand Alone," *The (Cleveland) Plain Dealer*, September 21, 1907, p. 12. Spalding was on hand to present a trophy to a school baseball team. At the beginning of his comments he asked for a show of hands of students interested in the game. "A little girl, flaxen haired and high browed," was the only dissenter.

14. "Spalding Back After Study of School Sports," *The Washington Times*, September 26, 1907, p. 10.

15. Sangree, loc. cit. Sangree expanded on this observation, first expressed in June 1907, later that year. See "Fans and Their Frenzies: The Wholesome Madness of Baseball," *Everybody's Magazine* 17 (September 1907), pp. 378-387, as reposted by John Thorn in his blog, *Our Game*, October 10, 2013, accessed January 4, 2025, at https://ourgame.mlblogs.com/fans-and-their-frenzies-the-wholesome-madness-of-baseball-476f34cd8389. There he wrote in part, "Now a young, ambitious and growing nation needs to 'let off steam.' Baseball furnishes the opportunity."

16. The contents of the issue are listed and summarized in "Baseball Magazine Proves to Be a Hit," *The Atlanta Journal*, May 23, 1908, p. 12.

Enter Tener

1. "New Ruler of Elks: John K. Tener, Once a Famous Baseball Star," *The Inquirer* (Lancaster, Pennsylvania), August 17, 1907, p. 2; "Tener Showed Eye for Business While Playing Baseball," *New Castle Herald*, April 16, 1908, p. 1; "Base-Ball Match," *Berrow's Worcester Journal* (England), March 16, 1889, p. 8.

2. No title, *The Manchester Guardian*, March 9, 1889, p. 9.

3. Ibid.

4. "New Ruler of Elks," op. cit.

5. "Ex-Governor Tener Dies at 82: Was National Figure in Politics, Sports," *The Pittsburgh Press*, May 20, 1946, pp. 1, 4' "John K. Tener Dead, Former Governor, Baseball Executive," *Pittsburgh Sun-Telegraph*, May 20, 1946, pp. 1, 2; "John Tener," SABR Bio Project, January 4, 2012, accessed July 1, 2024, at https://sabr.org/bioproj/person/john-tener/.

6. "John Tener," SABR Bio Project, op. cit.; and "Tener Once Fired: Wakened at Midnight and Told of Release," *The Wilkes-Barre Record*, December 12, 1910, p. 20. Statistics from "John Tener" on *Baseball Reference*, accessed July 1, 2024, at https://www.baseball-reference.com/register/player.fcgi?id=tener-002joh.

7. "New Ruler of Elks," op. cit.; "Tener Showed Eye for Business While Playing Baseball," *New Castle Herald*, April 16, 1908, p. 1; "Base-Ball Match," *Berrow's Worcester Journal* (England), March 16, 1889, p. 8.

8. "Base-Ball Match," op. cit.

9. "More Trouble in the Camp," *The Pittsburgh Post*, January 22, 1890, p. 6; and "Quite a Big Catch: John Tener Will Sign With Hanlon T-Day," *The Pittsburgh Dispatch*, February 19, 1890, p. 6.

10. "Hanlon's All Right," *The Pittsburgh Press*, October 5, 1890, p. 5.

11. See, for example, "John Tener on the Rubber," *The Pittsburgh Post*, April 27, 1899, p. 6.

12. "Want Him to Return: The Allegheny Athletic Association Making Efforts to Make John Tener an Amateur," *The Pittsburgh Dispatch*, January 22, 1891, p. 6.

13. "No Chance for John," *The Pittsburgh Dispatch*, January 31, 1891, p. 6.

14. "Multitude Turns Out to Witness Monster Parade," *The Pittsburgh Post*, November 3, 1907, pp. 1, 4, 5; "Bridge Plays Major Role in N. Charleroi's History," *Daily Republican* (Monongahela, Pennsylvania), July 11, 1969, p. 5; and "Bridge Opening to Be Big Event," *Pittsburgh Post-Gazette*, October 13, 1907, p. 15.

15. "John K. Tener Leads National Herd of Elks," *The Pittsburgh Post*, July 17, 1907, p. 1.

16. "High Officers Are Honored," *The Daily Times* (Davenport, Iowa), May 15, 1908, p. 1.

17. Ibid.

18. "Andrews Calls State Committee," *The Philadelphia Inquirer*, September 26, 1908, p. 7; "The Primary Law," *The New Castle Daily Herald*, April 14, 1908, p.4; and "John K. Tener Was in Town Last Night," *The Daily Republican* (Monongahela, Pennsylvania), April 10, 1908, p. 1.

19. "Fish Spares Not John Tener," *The New Castle Daily Herald*, October 13, 1908, p. 3; publication in the March 18, 1908, p. 7, issue of the same newspaper of Tener's letter; "Tener Says Fish's Statements And Arguments, in Part, Are False and Contrary to Reason," *The New Castle Daily Herald*, October 16, 1908, p. 1.; and *Canonsburg Daily Notes*, November 25, 1908, p. 4.

20. "Tener as a Candidate for Governor," *The New Castle Daily Herald*, December 17, 1908, p. 4.

The Tariff Tick-Tock

1. Cynthia G. Fox, "Income Tax Records of the Civil War Years," *Prologue Magazine*, Winter 1986, 18:4, passim.

2. Fisk, op. cit., p. 40.

3. See "Republican Party Platform of 1908," accessed June 10, 2024, at https://www.presidency.ucsb.edu/documents/republican-party-platform-1908. According to at least one observer, the ambiguity was widely perceived as "a promise to revise the tariff schedules downward, and a large proportion of the voters specifically voted for Republicans with this idea and expectation in mind." Edna Marie Griffin, *The Payne-Aldrich Tariff*, Master's Thesis, Loyola University Chicago, 1946, p. 34, accessed June 10, 2024, at https://ecommons.luc.edu/luc_theses/481. The point is reiterated in Fisk, op. cit., p. 37.

4. "Cannon is Named: Speaker Gets an Overwhelming Vote in House Caucus," *Washington Post*, March 14, 1909, p.1. It appears that Taft continued to struggle with the issue even after passage of the 1909 legislation. An indication of this is the extraordinarily long and detailed address he delivered, apparently in person, at Winona, Minnesota, on September 17, six weeks after its passage. See William Howard Taft, *Address on the Tariff Law of 1909*, found online June 10, 2024, at https://www.presidency.ucsb.edu/documents/address-the-tariff-law-1909. Clearly, however, his predecessor was not assuaged. It was in large measure on this difference of opinion that Roosevelt returned to challenge Taft's reelection in 1912, splitting the Republican vote and handing the presidency to Woodrow Wilson.

5. "Champ Clark Says Cannon Has Paresis," Louisville *Courier-Journal*, March 17, 1909, p. 5.

6. For a thorough legislative history of the legislation, see George M. Fisk, "The Payne-Aldrich Tariff," *Political Science Quarterly* 25:1 (March 1910), pp. 35-68. For the text of the Payne-Aldrich Act as finally adopted see Library of Congress, *Statutes at Large: Sixty-First Congress, Sess. I. Chap. 6. 1909.*, pp. 11-118, found online June 10, 2024, at https://maint.loc.gov/law/help/statutes-at-large/61st-congress/session-1/c61s1ch6.pdf. The length of this entry, all of it in single-spaced small print, only begins to suggest the complexity and degree of detail of this legislation. For an interesting comparison of tariff rates in Payne-Aldrich with those in the Underwood tariff bill of 1913, passed *after* the ratification of the Sixteenth Amendment, see *Protective Tariff Cyclopedia (Revised): The Payne-Aldrich Tariff Law of 1909 and Underwood Law of 1913 compared, giving every rate of duty in the laws of 1909 and 1913 and amendments of 1916* (New York: American Tariff League, 1918). Underwood amounted to a tax swap of sorts, reducing the average tariff rate on dutiable goods from between forty and fifty percent to less than twenty percent (declining by the decade's end) while at the same time imposing the nation's first tax on individual incomes with a top marginal rate of seven percent. See Phillip W. Magness, "The Problem of the Tariff in American Economic History, 1787-1934," *Globalization Then and Now* (Washington: CATO Institute Publications, September 26, 2023), p. 10.

7. In fairness, this was technically a special session, and the constitutionally mandated "First Session" did not convene until December, and then only briefly. But appointments remained within the purview of the Speaker and the Rules Committee nevertheless.

8. Data are drawn from the "Record of Climatological Observations" for Washington, DC, provided by the National Oceanic & Atmospheric Administration of the U.S. Department of Commerce, accessed August 6, 2024, at https://www.ncdc.noaa.gov/cdo-web/datasets/GHCND/stations/GHCND:USW00093725/detail.

9. "Mechanical refrigeration takes shape," *History of Air Conditioning*, U.S. Department of Energy, July 20, 2015, accessed August 6, 2024, at https://www.energy.gov/articles/history-air-conditioning; and "Capitol Power Plant: A Century of Service," Architect of the Capitol, December 5, 2010, accessed August 6, 2024, at https://www.aoc.gov/explore-capitol-campus/blog/capitol-power-plant-century-service#:~:text=In%201935%2C%20Congress%20appropriated%20funds,of%20the%20Washington%2C%20D.C.%20summers.

Mister Tener Goes to Washington

1. "Tener's Debut: The Ex-Pitcher Makes His First Appearance in Washington, Where He Will Be One of the Nation's Law-Makers, and Fans With Justice Moody," *Sporting Life*, March 13, 1909, p. 11; and "Old-Time Stars of the Diamond Now Shining at the Capitol," *The Pittsburgh Post*, December 12, 1908, p. 1.

2. *Index to the Congressional Record, Sixty-First Congress, First Session* (Washington: United States Congress, 1909), pp 446-447.

3. Voting data are drawn from "Rep. John Tener," accessed July 2, 2024, at https://www.govtrack.us/congress/members/john_tener/410707.

4. See, for example, the official website of the Congressional Baseball Game, accessed July 2, 2024, at https://www.congressionalbaseball.org/history/.

5. "Carnage: Is Something Awful When Those Big Swatting Democrats Cut Loose," *The Cincinnati Enquirer*, July 17, 1909, pp. 1-2; and "Solons to Play Ball," *The Washington Post*, July 10, 1909, p. 2.

6. "Solons to Play Ball," op. cit.

7. "Rep. Vreeland Is Doing Well," *Buffalo Evening News*, July 16, 1909, p. 1.

8. "Congressmen See Game," *The Washington Post*, June 24, 1909, p. 9.

9. See, for example, "Ford Car Wins Seattle Race: Makes Remarkable Cross-continental Run," *Los Angeles Times*, June 24, 1909, p. 7.

10. See the timetable from April 1909, accessed July 3, 2024, at https://www.annapolisrailroadhistory.com/washington-baltimore-annapolis-railroad-timetables.

11. "Congressmen on Tariff: Visitors to Baseball Game Talk Of 'Revision Downward,'" *The Baltimore Sun*, June 24, 1909, p. 12.

12. Headlines are from coverage on July 17, 1909, the day following the game.

Baseball in Washington

1. William Shakespeare, *A Midsummer Night's Dream*, II, i, 2.

2. "The Visit of the Union Club – Grand Match Game Yesterday," *The Washington Chronicle*, September 5, 1867, p. 1.

3. John Thorn, *Baseball in the Garden of Eden* (New York: Simon & Schuster, 2011), pp. 136-140.

4. "Base Ball: Grand Match at Cedar Hill," *The Courier-Journal*, July 17, 1867, p. 3.

5. "The National Baseball Club," *The National Republican* (Washington, D.C.), July 20, 1867, p. 3.

6. "Base Ball in the C. A. C.," *The Washington Sunday Herald*, February 8, 1891, p. 8.

7. "In on the Ground Floor," *The Washington Sunday Herald*, January 18, 1891, p. 5.

8. "A Meeting of Base Ball Backers," *The Washington Evening Star*, December 5, 1890, p.3; and "A Creditable Victory: The Nationals Down the Baltimores at Their First Meeting," *The Washington Sunday Herald*, April 19, 1891, p. 8.

9. The outlines of this history are found in "Washington Baseball Timeline," accessed July 4, 2024, at https://www.mlb.com/nationals/history/timeline-1859-1959; and "Timeline of Major League Baseball," accessed July 4, 2024, at https://en.wikipedia.org/wiki/Timeline_of_Major_League_Baseball.

10. "Presidents Attended Games Long Ago," *The Washington Evening Star*, April 25, 1909, p. 4.

11. While the specifics of certain venues are sourced elsewhere here, the general identification of field locations is enlightened by "Washington Played Here," *The Washington Post*, March 27, 2008, accessed July 4, 2024, at https://www.washingtonpost.com/wp-dyn/content/article/2008/03/27/AR2008032703101.html.

12. "Base-Ball," *The National Republican* (Washington, D.C.), April 15, 1867, p. 3.

13. "New Government Printing Office Site," *The Washington Evening Star*, January 7, 1891, p. 6; and "The Government Printing Office: Report of the Committee to Select a Site – The Old Base Ball Grounds," *The Washington Evening Star*, February 26, 1891, p. 5.

14. "Baseball Men in Session," *The Washington Evening Star*, January 13, 1891, p. 5.

15. "We Are In It: Washington's Brilliant Base Ball Prospects for Next Year," *The Washington Evening Star*, January 17, 1891, p. 6.

16. "In on the Ground Floor," *The Washington Sunday Herald*, January 18, 1891, p. 5.

17. "Base-Ball News Scarce," *The Washington Sunday Herald*, January 25, 1891, p. 8.

18. "New Base Ball Grounds," *The Washington Evening Star*, January 30, 1891, p. 8.

19. "Fine Base Ball Outlook," *The Washington Sunday Herald*, February 1, 1891, p. 5.

20. "Dunlap Will Be a Senator," *The Washington Evening Star*, February 5, 1891, p. 5.

21. W. Montague Cobb, M.D., "A Short History of Freedmen's Hospital," *Journal of the National Medical Association* 54:3 (May 1962), pp. 271-287.

22. "The Base-Ball Situation," *The Washington Sunday Herald*, February 8, 1891, p. 8.

23. "Hopes For a Good Ball Team," *The Washington Evening Star*, February 7, 1891, p. 11.

24. "Washington Corporations," *The Washington Evening Star*, February 9, 1891, p. 6.

25. Classified advertisement, *The Washington Evening Star*, February 12, 1891, p. 2.

26. "What Will the Team Be?" *The Washington Evening Star*, February 14, 1891, p. 12.

27. "General Sporting Gossip: The Permit Granted," *The Washington Sunday Herald*, February 15, 1891, p. 15.

28. "District Government: The Base Ball Park Permit Granted, *The Washington Evening Star*, February 16, 1891, p. 5.

29. "The Fight Is On," *The Washington Evening Star*, February 19, 1891, p. 6.

30. "The Base Ball War," *The Washington Evening Standard*, February 28, 1891, p. 11.

31. "Washington Played Here," op. cit.

32. "New Base Ball Plans," *The Washington Evening Star*, March 3, 1891, p. 5; "Allen W. Thurman," *Baseball reference*, accessed July 12, 2024, at https://www.baseball-reference.com/bullpen/Allen_W._Thurman.

33. "Getting Everything Ready," *The Washington Evening Star*, March 7, 1891, p. 14.

34. "City and District: Base Ball Talk," *The Washington Evening Star*, March 23, 1891, p. 7.

35. "If It Shouldn't Rain: Washington Will See the First Game To-Morrow," *The Washington Sunday Herald*, April 12, 1891, p. 5.

36. "The Nationals Neatly Shut Out By the Boston Hard Hitters," *The Washington Evening Star*, April 14, 1891, p. 6.

37. Classified advertisement in *The Washington Evening Star*, July 27, 1895, p. 10.

38. "Down to Business: Local Base Ball Syndicate Calls a Meeting for Tomorrow Night," *The Washington Evening Star*, November 15, 1899, p. 14.

39. "The Baseball Outlook: Many Questions to be Decided at the Meeting of Magnates," *The Washington Evening Times*, December 11, 1899, p. 6.

40. "Senators in League," *The Washington Post*, January 28, 1900, p. 8.

41. "Earl Wagner Speaks: Says Washington Was Forced Out of League," *The Washington Post*, February 13, 1900, p. 8.

42. "Sports in General," *The Washington Evening Star*, November 23, 1900, p. 10.

43. "Ban Johnson Coming," *The Washington Post*, January 17, 1901, p. 8.

44. "Manning's Great Coup: Fell Like a Wet Blanket Over Major League Circuit," *The Washington Post*, February 17, 1901, p. 8.

45. "At Work on American League Park," *The Washington Post*, February 21, 1901, p. 8.

46. "Play on Georgetown Field," *The Washington Post*, April 18, 1901, p. 9.

47. "First Game Today: New American Park Completed and Ready for the Public," *The Washington Evening Star*, April 29, 1901, p. 9.

48. "President Johnson Outlines Plans for Senators," *The Washington Evening Star*, March 9, 1904, p. 9.

49. "Hostile to Ball Park," *The Washington Post*, March 25, 1904, p. 12.

50. "Base Ball Enthusiasts Pleased with Senators' Sale," *The Washington Evening Star*, March 24, 1904, p. 9; and "Senators Will Play on the Old Grounds," *The Washington Times*, March 27, 1904, p. 9.

51. "Work to Begin on Ball Park," *The Washington Times*, March 29, 1904, p. 8; and "Ball Park Injunction: Brick Company and Club Owners Sign Papers and Work May Begin To-Day," *The Washington Post*, March 30, 1904.

52. "Tearing Down the Stands," *The Washington Post*, March 31, 1904, p. 9.

CBG1: Scheduling the Game

1. "Dispute Over Pitcher," *The Washington Herald*, January 24, 1909, p. 9; and "Piedmont White Sox Organize," *The Washington Herald*, February 18, 1909, p. 8.

2. "Amateur Baseball," *The Washington Post*, April 11, 1909, p. 2.

3. "Form New Ball League," *The Washington Post*, December 17, 1907.

4. "Signs Five Players: Manager Irwin Lays Nucleus of Outlaw Club," *The Washington Herald*, March 19, 1908, p. 8; and Unions Arrive To-Day," *The Washington Post*, April 16, 1908, p. 8.

5. "Al Lawson Is Satisfied: Union Baseball League President Confident of Success Here," *The Washington Herald*, March 29, 1908, p. 9.

6. "Local Club Dissolved: Outlaw Baseball Ends Short Lived Career Here," *The Washington Post*, June 4, 1908, p. 8.

7. Advertisement, *The Washington Evening Star*, April 25, 1909, p. 4.

8. Washington Giants Win," *The Washington Herald*, August 31, 1909, p. 8.

9. "Royal Giants Beat Philadelphia Giants," *The Washington Post*, September 16, 1909, p. 8.

10. "Fifth Game of Series," *The Washington Herald*, August 22, 1909, p. 2.

11. "Two Games at Ball Park," *The Washington Evening Star*, July 4, 1909, p. 4.

12. "In Amateur Baseballdom," *The Washington Post*, April 24, 1909, p. 9.

13. "Amateur Season a Very Big Success," *The Washington Evening Star*, August 15, 1909, Part 5, p. 3; and "Baseball, Racing and Other Sports," *The Washington Evening Star*, June 30, 1909, p. 20.

14. "Separate Battalion's Annual review Tomorrow," *The Washington Evening Star*, May 24, 1909, p. 4; "Won By the 'Babies': New Company E Takes Colored Cadets' Drill Prize," *The Washington Evening Star*, May 26, 1909, p. 13; and "Newcomers Win Drill," *The Washington Post*, May 27, 1909, p. 4.

15. "High School Men in Prize Drills," *The Washington Herald*, May 19, 1909, p. 1.

16. "Getting Ready for Football: George Washington Team to Play at American League Park," *The Washington Evening Star*, June 30, 1909, p. 20. Game results found at "1909 George Washington Hatchetites Football Team," accessed August 10, 2024, at https://en.wikipedia.org/wiki/1909_George_Washington_Hatchetites_football_team.

Senators Joint Irresolution (S. J. I. 18)

1. "Baseball Notes," *The Washington Post*, June 7, 1904, p. 8.

2. On the weather in Detroit, see "Detroit Weather in 1909," accessed July 8, 2024, at https://www.extremeweatherwatch.com/cities/detroit/year-1909. On Bennett Park see "Bennett Park (Detroit)," accessed July 8, 2024, at https://en.wikipedia.org/wiki/Bennett_Park_(Detroit). The account of the ballgame that follows is based on the following: "Eighteen Innings with Nary a Run Record Base Ball," *The Washington Evening Star*, July 17, 1909, p. 8; "Nationals and Tigers Play 18-Inning Tie in which Neither Score," *The Washington Post*, July 17, 1909, p.8; "Nationals Play for 18 Innings," *The Washington Herald*, July 17, 1909, pp. 1, 8; "All Records Broken for Scoreless Play," *The Detroit Free Press*, July 17, 1909, p. 1, 8; and "Batters the Goats Before Pitchers in Swell Game," *The Detroit Times*, July 17, 1909, p.6.

The Thrill Up on The Hill

1. "Members of House to Play Baseball," *The Washington Herald*, July 11, 1909, p. 2; and "Lawmakers Play Ball for Charity," *The Washington Times*, July 16, 1909, p. 10.

2. "Greater Issue Than the Tariff," *The Boston Globe*, July 16, 1909, p. 8.

3. "Rep. Vreeland Is Doing Well," *Buffalo Evening News*, July 16, 1909, p. 1; and "Disabled: In Ball Game Practice," *The Cincinnati Enquirer*, July 16, 1909, p. 3.

4. The account of the game that follows is based on an amalgam of the information, often overlapping, provided in the following sources: "Democrats Win Real Ball Game," *The Washington Herald*, July 17, 1909, pp. 1, 9; "Carnage Is Something Awful When Those Big Swatting Democrats Cut Loose: Republican Ball Team Ground into Dust," *The Cincinnati Enquirer*, July 17, 1909, pp. 1, 2; "Democrats Win Baseball Game," *The Philadelphia Inquirer*, July 17, 1909, p. 4; "Arkansas, Alabama and Tennessee Stars, Who Figured in the Recent Congressional Baseball Game," *The Commercial Appeal* (Memphis, Tennessee), July 23, 1909, p. 8; "Democrats Score Their Only Victory of the Extra Session," *Nashville Banner*, July 17, 1909, p. 3; "Solons Play Ball," *The Washington Post*, July 17, 1909, pp. 1, 4; "List of Cripples Numbers Twenty," *The Washington Times*, July 17, 1909, p. 4; Mary Craig, "A Comedy of Errors: The First Congressional Baseball Game," *The Hardball Times*, April 10, 2017, accessed July 9, 2024, at https://tht.fangraphs.com/a-comedy-of-errors-the-first-congressional-baseball-game/; and Robert Pohl, "Lost Capitol Hill: The First Congressional Baseball Game," February 27, 2012, accessed July 11, 2024, at https://thehillishome.com/2012/02/lost-capitol-hill-the-first-congressional-baseball-game/. Additional citations, including duplicates, added as appropriate.

5. "Carnage Is Something Awful," op. cit., p. 1.

6. "Democrats Win Ball Game," *The New York Sun*, July 17, 1909, p. 2.

7. Mary Craig, ibid.; and "Presidents Attended Games Long Ago," op. cit.

8. "Rain Helps Tie Game," *The Washington Post*, May 21, 1910, p. 8.

9. "Won By Home-Run Hit," *The Washington Post*, June 12, 1897, p. 8; Billy Evans, "Bleacher Fan Ranks First as Game's Leading Critic," *The Washington Star*, January 25, 1914, Part 5, p. 4; and "Diamond Dust," *The Washington Times*, July 25, 1898, p. 6; "Death Calls Jim O'Day, Popular Nat Employe," *The Washington Post*, November 15, 1926, p. 11.

10. "The Rev. James A. Reynolds," *Newark Evening Star*, May 26, 1914, p. 2; "Present Watch to Fr. Reynolds on Silver Jubilee," *The Newark Evening Star*, August 24, 1910, p. 4; and "Priest at Red Bank Honored," *Perth Amboy Evening News*, August 25, 1910, p. 3.

11. "Carnage," op. cit., p. 1.

12. "Real Baseball in Congress," *The Inter Ocean* (Chicago), July 18, 1909, p. 6.

13. "Baseball Victory for the Democrats," *The New York Times*, July 17, 1909, p. 2; and "Solons Play Ball," op. cit., p. 1.

Sturm und Drang

1. "Lightning Strikes Washington Homes: Freak Storm Wreaks Damage in Center of City," *The Washington Herald*, July 17, 1909, pp. 1, 3; and "Rain Drenches City," *The Washington Evening Star*, July 17, 1909, p. 6.

2. "Rain Prevents Flight," *The Washington Herald*, July 17, 1909, p. 3; and "Wrights See Jonah," *The Washington Post*, July 17, 1909, p. 1-2.

3. "Curtiss in Flight: Competitor of Wright Brothers After Big Prize," *The Washington Examiner*, July 17, 1909; and "Curtiss Flies 31 Minutes," *The Washington Post*, July 17, 1909, p. 2.

4. "Wrights See Jonah," op. cit.; and "Bolt Stuns Phone User: Well-Known Alexandrian Shocked and Burned," *The Washington Post*, July 17, 1909, p. 3.

5. "List of Cripples Numbers Twenty," op. cit.

Past As Prologue: Life After CBG1

1. Joseph Postell, "Speaker Joseph Cannon Dethroned," Bill of Rights Institute, ND, accessed July 15, 2024, at https://billofrightsinstitute.org/essays/speaker-joseph-cannon-dethroned.

2. *Congressional Record*, House of Representatives, March 19, 1910, p. 3425.

3. "Fowler Revives Insurgent Fight," *The Washington Herald*, April 22, 1910, p. 4.

4. Postell, op. cit.

5. Though Garner made a number of disparaging remarks about the vice presidency, there is uncertainty as to whether he made this one. It is, nevertheless, widely attributed to him. For a discussion of this point, see Patrick Cox, "John Nance Garner on the Vice Presidency – In Search of the Proverbial Bucket," Briscoe Center for American History, accessed August 10, 2024, at https://briscoecenter.org/about/news/john-nance-garner-on-the-vice-presidency-in-search-of-the-proverbial-bucket/.

6. "Priest at Red Bank Honored," op. cit.

7. "Father Reynolds Dead," *Red Bank Register*, May 27, 1914, p. 9.

8. "Carpenters Busy At Baseball Park," *The Washington Times*, March 13, 1911, p. 10.

9. "Grandstand and Bleachers Go in Mysterious Fire At Ball Grounds," *The Washington Times*, March 17, 1911, pp. 1-2.

10. Classified advertisement, *The Washington Herald*, March 21, 1911, p. 10.

11. "Busy At Ball Park: New Stands Are Being Rushed Rapidly to Completion," *The Washington Post*, April 2, 1911, p. 3; and "Box Seats on Sale Tuesday Morning," *The Washington Star*, April 9, 1911, p. 57; and Baseball Grounds Mecca for Many Thousands of Fans," *The Washington Times*, April 9, 1911, p. 16.

12. "Johnson Here and Nationals Face Red Sox," *The Washington Times*, April 12, 1911, pp. 1, 17.

13. "Local American League Club May Put Tickets on Sale Next Season Downtown," *The Washington Times*, December 30, 1911, p. 10.

14. "New Groundkeeper for Local Ball Park Is Signed," *The Washington Evening Star*, January 6, 1912, p. 10.

15. "Freezing Weather Halts Work At Nat Stadium," *The Washington Post*, January 3, 1926.

16. "Ground-Keeper O'Day Suffers Heart Spell," *The Washington Post*, January 12, 1926, p. 18; and "Death Calls Jim O'Day, Popular Nat Employe," *The Washington Post*, November 15, 1926, p. 11.

17. "Nationals Smothered in Final Game at New York: Game Degenerates Into Farce," *The Washington Post*, April 25, 1909, Sporting Section, p. 1.

18. See, for example, "Taft Will Sign Tariff Bill," *The New York Sun*, July 26, 1909, p. 10.

19. For the full text of the final bill, see *Public Acts of the Sixty-First Congress of the United States*, Session I, Chapters 2-4, 6, pp. 11-118. Taft later made an extraordinary effort to explain his support of the bill in a detailed address he delivered on September 17 in Winona, Minnesota. See William Howard Taft, "Address on the Tariff Law of 1909," accessed July 25, 2024, at https://www.presidency.ucsb.edu/documents/address-the-tariff-law-1909.

20. "Ax for Insurgents: Speaker Wields It in Naming New Committees," *The Washington Post*, August 6, 1909, pp. 1, 4.

21. The debate on the final version of the bill, as amended by the Senate, began on page 5088 of the *Congressional Record* and concluded on page 5091. Thereupon the Speaker read into the record a brief letter from a Member who had been absent due to a health emergency and another from his physician certifying the same. That was followed immediately by two pages listing the creation of every committee of the House and the names of every Member who had been appointed to each. *Congressional Record – House* Vol. 44, Part 5, (Washington: United States Congress), August 5, 1909, pp. 5088-5093.

22. *Protective Tariff Cyclopedia* (revised) (New York: American Protective Tariff League, 1918), pp. 3-149.

23. "Would Mop Up the Field With Republicans," *The Pittsburgh Press*, July 16, 1909, p. 11.

24. "Mr. Taft in Doubt," *The Washington Post*, June 17, 1910, p. 4.

25. "Tener Withdraws Nomination," *The Washington Post*, July 27, 1910, p. 1; and "Up to Dr. Dixon Can Succeed Himself," *Franklin Repository* (Chambersburg, Pennsylvania), November 16, 1910, p. 1.

26. "Ex-Governor Tener Dies at 82: Was National Figure in Politics, Sports," *The Pittsburgh Press*, May 20, 1946, pp. 1, 4; and "John K. Tener Dead: Former Governor, Baseball Executive," *The Pittsburgh Sun-Telegraph*, May 20, 1946, pp. 1-2.

27. "Governor Tener Will Free Baseball in Penna. From Gambling Abuses," *The Harrisburg Telegraph*, March 30, 1912, p. 1.

28. "Governor Tener is Commended," *The Harrisburg Telegraph*, April 8, 1912, p. 8. For an example of related coverage, see "Betting on Baseball," *The New York Times*, March 31, 1912, p. 35.

29. "Nationwide Campaign Against Base Ball Pools," *The Wilkes-Barre Semi-Weekly Record*, June 1, 1915, p. 7.

30. "Tener to Lead the League," *The Cincinnati Enquirer*, November 6, 1913, p. 6.

31. "John K. Tener: Governor of Pennsylvania Who May Head National League," *The Allentown Leader*, November 8, 1913, p. 16.

32. "Pennsylvania Governor Chosen President of National League," *The Washington Herald*, December 10, 1913, p. 10.

33. William A. Phelon, "The Treaty of Cincinnati," *Baseball Magazine*, February 1916, pp. 15-22, passim. The quotation appears on p. 16.

34. F.C. Lane, "Has President Tener Made Good?" *Baseball Magazine*, April 1916, pp. 62-66.

35. "Ex-Governor Tener Dies at 82," op. cit.

36. "Congressmen in a Hurry for School to Let Out," *The Atlanta Journal*, August 8, 1911, p. 15.

37. "Odor of Liniment Reigns Over House in Wake of Game," *The Washington Times*, August 8, 1911, p. 3; "Democrats Win Base Ball Game," *The Bluff City News* (Kansas), August 11, 1911, p. 7; "Congressional Ball Game," *The Washington Post*, August 6, 1911, p. 2; and "Congressmen in a Hurry For School to Let Out," *The Atlanta Journal*, August 8, 1911, p. 15. The box score of the abbreviated contest was reported in "Congressional Game," *Sporting Life*, August 12, 1911, p. 6. It is possible that the game had been postponed from an earlier date, which may account for the change of venue. In "House Ball Game Today," *The Washington Post*, July 22, 1911, p. 5, indicated that the game was to be played on that date at American League Park, which as we know, did not happen. That same issue of the *Post* reported that heavy local rains were expected in the Mid-Atlantic area (p. 2).

CBG: The Legacy

1. Personal correspondence with Ryan Thompson, president of the foundation. The 2024 list of sponsors was accessed March 7, 2025, at https://www.congressionalbaseball.org/sponsors/.

2. "Wins & Losses Through the Years," History, Art & Archives, United States House of Representatives, accessed June 26, 2024, at https://history.house.gov/Exhibitions-and-Publications/Baseball-Game/Statistics/.

3. "The Players," History, Art & Archives, United States House of Representatives, accessed June 26, 2024, at https://history.house.gov/Exhibitions-and-Publications/Baseball-Game/Players/. The names identified by the House as former professional baseball players were checked against the records maintained by Baseball-Reference.com, which maintains a definitive database of both major and minor league professional players throughout the history of the game, with the results as reported.

4. "Baseball Firsts & Notables," History, Art & Archives, United States House of Representatives, accessed June 26, 2024, at https://history.house.gov/Exhibitions-and-Publications/Baseball-Game/Fanfare/.

5. Alexander Comisar, "100 Years of Congressional Baseball," *Roll Call*, June 16, 2009.

6. "Deirdre Shesgreen, Jessie Balmert, and Chrissie Thompson, "Wenstrup Comes to Scalise's Aid," Mansfield, Ohio, *News Journal*, June 15, 2024, p. B3; and Kevin Johnson and Ray Locker, "Scalise Shooter

Raged on Facebook," Mansfield, Ohio, *News Journal*, June 15, 2024, p. B3.

7. Comisar, op. cit.

The Last Act (Literally)

1. "Another Credit Mobilier?" *The Vicksburg Herald*, August 8, 1909, p. 5.

2. "Risk Chief Is Arrested: H.M. Coudrey, Former Congressman, Taken in New York on Fraud Charge," *Genoa Republican-Journal* (Illinois), November 10, 1911, p. 2.

3. "Of Interest to District," *The Washington Post*, August 6, 1909, p. 4. See also *Congressional Record - House*, Vol. 44, Part 5, August 5, 1909, p. 5096.

Choosing Sides

1. William T. Kirk, "Choosing Sides," *Sporting Life*, June 3, 1911, p.5.

Appendix 1: The Players

1. Biographical information is amalgamated from the *Biographical Directory of the United States Congress*, Wikipedia, and other sources as indicated.

Appendix 2: The Tariff Reform Calendar

1. "History of Bills and Resolutions," H.R. 1438, *Congressional Record Index*, Sixty-First Congress, First Session, p. 119.

Appendix 4: History of the Congressional Baseball Game

1. "Wins & Losses Through the Years," History, Art & Archives, United States House of Representatives, accessed June 26, 2024, at https://history.house.gov/Exhibitions-and-Publications/Baseball-Game/Statistics/.

ACKNOWLEDGMENTS

AS ALWAYS, I have benefited greatly in writing this book from the assistance and suggestions of others. So . . . Special thanks to my good friend Al Arrighi for his careful reading of an early manuscript and his good suggestions, and to Frank Amoroso for the same. Thanks as well to baseball historian Dr. Gary Livacari, editor of the Baseball History Comes Alive website, and researcher Don Stokes for identifying the players and others in the opening day photograph of the 1909 Washington Nationals, as well as Ryan Thompson, founder and president of the Congressional Sports for Charity Foundation, for his interest and updates on the latest developments. And a special shoutout to Lawrence Knorr, baseball historian, polymath, graphic artist, IT whiz, and not incidentally, founder and CEO of Sunbury Press, for converting a collection of old congressional portraits into some really cool period-looking baseball cards. Lawrence did double duty here, serving as well as editor of this opus, and he created the cover art. Thanks as well to others on the great crew at Sunbury. This is my eighth book with that house, and every one of them has benefited not only from LK's eye for a good story but also from Crystal Devine's divine design sense. Katie Cressman's more recent and welcome addition to the team has helped to keep the wheels turning smoothly.

Finally, I want to thank once again my personal editor-in-chief and toughest critic, not to mention my wife and helpmate of fifty-five-plus years, Amy. As it says at the top of this book, she still bats a round grand. And she can probably pitch, too.

SELECTED SOURCES CONSULTED

Achorn, Edward. *The Summer of Beer and Whiskey*. New York: Public Affairs, 2013.

Adams, Charles. *When in the Course of Human Events: Arguing the Case for Southern Secession*. Lanham, MD: Rowman & Littlefield, 2000.

American Protective Tariff League. *Protective Tariff Cyclopedia*, Revised. New York, 1918.

Ceresi, Frank, and Mark Rucker. *Baseball in Washington, D.C.* Charleston, SC: Arcadia Publishing, 2002.

Cobb, W. Montague, M.D., "A Short History of Freedmen's Hospital," *Journal of the National Medical Association* 54:3 (May 1962), pp. 271-287.

Comisar, Alexander, "100 Years of Congressional Baseball," *Roll Call*, June 16, 2009.

Craig, Mary. "A Comedy of Errors: The First Congressional Baseball Game," *Hardball Times*, April 10, 2017, accessed July 9, 2024, at https://tht.fangraphs.com/a-comedy-of-errors-the-first-congressional-baseball-game/.

Hagerty, Tim. *Tales from the Dugout: 1,001 Humorous, Inspirational & Wild Anecdotes from Minor League Baseball*. Nashville, TN: Cider Mill Press, 2023.

Koszarek, Ed. *The Players League: History, Clubs, Ballplayers and Statistics*. Jefferson, NC: McFarland & Company, 2006.

Levine, Peter. *A.G. Spalding and the Rise of Baseball*. New York: Oxford University Press, 1985.

Magness, Phillip W. "The Problem of the Tariff in American Economic History, 1787-1934," Cato Institute, September 26, 2023.

Morris, Peter. *Level Playing Fields: How the Groundskeeping Murphy Brothers Shaped Baseball*. Lincoln: University of Nebraska Press, 2007.

Sarnoff, Gary. *Team of Destiny: Walter Johnson, Clark Griffith, Bucky Harris and the 1924 Washington Senators*. Lanham, MD: Rowman & Littlefield, 2024.

Tarbell, Ida M. *The Tariff in Our Times*. New York: McMillan, 1911.

Wallace, Richard, and Marie Pinak Carr. *The Willard Hotel: An Illustrated History*. Washington, DC: Dicmar Publishing, 1986.

Wiggins, Robert Peyton. *The Federal League of Base Ball Clubs*. Jefferson, NC: McFarland & Company, 2009.

Wolf, Gregory H., ed. *Griffith Stadium: A Palace in the Nation's Capital*. Phoenix, AZ: Society for American Baseball Research, 2021.

ART CREDITS

NUMBERED FIGURES

Figure 1. Charting the Biggest Pickle in Baseball History (1909). The Washington Post, August 15, 1909, p. 3.

Figure 2. Oriole Park IV (1909). This rare photograph of Orioles Park IV was taken in 1909 after the ballpark was realigned relative to Greenmount Street. Photo courtesy of David Stinson and Bernard McKenna.

Figure 3. The English View of Baseball. No title, *The Manchester Guardian,* March 9, 1889, p. 9.

Figure 4. Just What the Doctor Ordered? This cartoon by an artist identified only as Hartman appeared on the cover of *Sporting Life* 29:8, May 15, 1897.

Figure 5. Daily Schedule of Washington-Baltimore Rail Service (1909). https///www.an napolisrailroadhistory.com/washington-baltimore-annapolis-railroad-timetables.

Figure 6. Baseball was still played on the Ellipse (The White Lot) in 1945. Library of Congress Catalog. https://www.loc.gov/resource/fsa.8e07378/.

Figure 7. Washington, DC, Map Showing Street Rail Lines (1895). Library of Congress Catalog. https://www.loc.gov/item/87695721/.

Figure 8. A Game at American League Park, Washington, DC (1905). Library of Congress Catalog. https://www.loc.gov/item/2007664602/.

Figure 9. Map Showing Location of American League Park (1909). Baist's Real Estate Atlas of Surveys of Washington, District of Columbia, Vol. 3, Plate 17. *Library of Congress Catalog.* https://www.loc.gov/resource/g3851bm.gct00133c/?sp=21&r=-0.07,0.035,1.171,0.791,0.

Figure 10. Opening Day, 1909. Library of Congress Catalog. https://www.loc.gov/ item/96518309/. Identification of players courtesy of Gary Livacari.

Figure 11. "Uncle Joe" Cannon (left), Speaker of the House, whose purple socks are not shown here. The Washington Times, July 17, 1909, p.4.

Figure 12. The Umpires: Jim O'Day and Rev. James Reynolds. The Washington Times, March 13, 1911, p. 10 (O'Day); *The Newark Star-Eagle,* August 24, 1910, p. 24 (Reynolds).

Figure 13. The Democratic Contestants. The Washington Post, July 17, 1909. p. 4.

Figure 14. The Republican Contestants. The Washington Post, July 17, 1909. p. 4.

Figure 15. You Can't Tell the Players Without a Cartoon. The Washington Herald, July 17, 1909, p. 1.

Figure 16. Game Action. The Commercial Appeal (Memphis), July 23, 1909, p. 8.

Figure 17. The Box Score of CBG1. The Washington Herald, July 17, 1909, p. 9.

Figure 18. Map of the Area Affected By the Freak Storm of July 16, 1909. Chicago: Rand McNally, c. 1909. *Library of Congress Catalog.* https://www.loc.gov/ item/87691456/.

Figure 19. The Survivors. The Washington Evening Star, July 17, 1909, p. 1.

Figure 20. Roosevelt Plays the Spoiler. 1912 Postcard, signed by artist "Allan."

Figure 21. Preparing the Field, Removing Lumber From the Stands, April 8, 1911. The Washington Times, April 8, 1911, p. 10.

Figure 22. National Park Opening Day 1911. The Washington Times, April 9, 1911, p. 1.

Figure 23. Page of the Congressional Record from August 5, 1909. Congressional Record – House, August 5, 1909, p. 5091.

Figure 24. The 1911 Republican Team for CBG2. Photo By Harris & Ewing. *Library of Congress Catalog.* https://www.loc.gov/item/2016863421/, February 17, 2024.

PLAYER PHOTOGRAPHS

Garrett (circa 1915): LC-B2- 6182-8 [P&P]. Library of Congress Prints and Photographs Division Washington, D.C. 20540. Digital ID: ggbain 37056. Control Number: ggb2006012469. Reproduction Number: LC-DIG-ggbain-37056.

Heflin (1905): Photo by Harris & Ewing. *Library of Congress Catalog:* https://www.loc. gov/pictures/item/2016861288/.

Hughes (1912): *Library of Congress Catalog:* https://lccn.loc.gov/2005689530

McDermott (ND): Photo by Harris & Ewing. *Library of Congress Catalog:* https://www. loc.gov/pictures/item/2016858489/.

Oldfield (ND): Photo by Harris & Ewing. *Library of Congress Catalog:* https://loc.gov/ pictures/resource/hec.16257/.

Kinkead (circa 1940): Photo by Harris & Ewing. https://commons.wikimedia.org/ wiki/File:Eugene_Francis_Kinkead.jpg#filehistory.

Robinson (2012): Photo by Harris & Ewing. https://commons.wikimedia.org/wiki/ File:Joseph_T._Robinson_cropped.jpg.

Driscoll (ND): Collection of the U.S. House of Representatives. https://bioguide .congress.gov/search/bio/D000500.

O'Connell (circa 1908): Luther Stearns Cushing, *Who's Who in State Politics, 1908.* (Reprinted by Forgotten Books, 2020). https://commons.wikimedia.org/wiki/ File:Joseph_F._O%27Connell_Massachusetts_Congressman_circa_1908.png.

Webb (ND): Photo by Bain News Service. *Library of Congress Catalog:* hdl.loc.gov/loc. pnp/ggbain.12921.

Thomas (1906): William Alexander Taylor, *The Biographical Annals of Ohio, 1902-: A Handbook of the Government and Institutions of the State of Ohio,* Vol. 3, p. 800.

Cole (1900): Photo by Bain News Service. *Library of Congress Catalog.* http://hdl.loc. gov/loc.pnp/ggbain.02562.

Dawson (1913): *The History of the First National Bank in the United States: A History of the First National Bank of Davenport, Iowa, Preceded by Some Account of Banking Under State Laws and Early Banking in Davenport.* Chicago: Rand McNally, 1913), following p. 144.

Tener (1910): Photo by J. Gutekunst. *Library of Congress Catalog*: http://hdl.loc.gov/loc.pnp/cph.3b02037.

Tener Baseball Card (1887-1890): Issued by Goodwyn & Company. *Library of Congress Catalog.* https://www.loc.gov/resource/bbc.0158f/.

Howland (ND): Photo by Harris & Ewing. *Library of Congress Catalog.* https://www.loc.gov/pictures/item/2016858228/.

Ames (1908): Source Unknown. https://commons.wikimedia.org/wiki/File:Butler_Ames_Massachusetts_Congressman.png.

Longworth (1920): Photo by National Photo Company. *Library of Congress Catalog.* https://lccn.loc.gov/2016827928.

Burke (1901): Percy Frazer Smith, *Notable Men of Pittsburgh and Vicinity.* Pittsburgh Printing Company, 1901, p. 399. *Library of Congress Catalog.* https://www.loc.gov/resource/gdcmassbookdig.notablemenofpitt01smit/?sp=403&st=image&r=-0.126,0.271,1.396,1.201,0.

Gaines (ND): Photo by Harris & Ewing. *Library of Congress Catalog.* https://loc.gov/pictures/resource/hec.20306/.

Vreeland (1908): Photo by Bain News Service. *Library of Congress Catalog.* https://loc.gov/pictures/resource/ggbain.01214/.

INDEX

ABOUT THE AUTHOR

J.B. MANHEIM is the award-winning author of The Deadball Files, a series of present-day mysteries and legal thrillers grounded in events and personalities of the Deadball Era in baseball, the years between 1900 and 1920. Books in the series have scored highly in national competitions, and one title, *The Federal Case*, was judged the Best Legal Thriller in the 2024 American Fiction Awards. His one previous nonfiction baseball title, the best-selling *What's in Ted's Wallet? The Newly Revealed T206 Baseball Card Collection of Thomas Edison's Youngest Son*, co-authored with Lawrence Knorr, was featured in 2024 at the annual Edison Day celebration at the Thomas Edison National Historical Park.

An expert in strategic communication in politics, Manheim is Professor Emeritus at George Washington University, where he developed the world's first degree-granting program in political communication and was later founding director of the School of Media & Public Affairs. He is a past chair of the Political Communication Section of the American Political Science Association and was the 1995 Professor of the Year for the District of Columbia. He learned his love of baseball long ago playing catch with his father in the backyard, acquiring splinters in Little League, singing along to "The Wabash Cannonball" with Dizzy Dean on black and white *Game of the Week* broadcasts, and freezing through cold July nights with his grandfather at the Mistake By the Lake, also known as Cleveland Municipal Stadium.

www.ingramcontent.com/pod-product-compliance
Lightning Source LLC
Chambersburg PA
CBHW011155090426
42740CB00018B/3395